America Misunderstood

What a Second Bush Victory Meant to the Rest of the World

Published by: DivineTree Publications – A division of Zpole LLC
Bridgewater, NJ 08807 USA
www.divinetree.com
info@divinetree.com

Distributed and Marketed by Midpoint Trade Books
New York, NY 10011

ISBN 0-9755140-1-6

Library of Congress Control Number (PCN): 2006907990

Cover design by Infinite Media.

Printed in the United States of America.

To those journalists who risk their lives to report the truth

CONTENTS

Introduction

A friend of mine regularly sends me a little-known literary
magazine called *Nandalala*, published from a remote part of
central Sri Lanka. The magazine—which barely has a circulation of
500 copies among a small, underprivileged Indian immigrant community nestled in the colonial tea plantations—helps me keep in
touch with the literary happenings and developments around the
town where I grew up, where the Internet has yet to make inroads.

A year ago, I received a copy of the magazine that shocked me
and sent shivers down my spine.

The theme of that issue was Iraq!

I couldn't believe my eyes. The people of Sri Lanka have more
than enough to write about: poverty, human rights violations,
oppression by political forces, child labor, women's rights, and so on.
Why write about Iraq? I was puzzled.

I skimmed through the pages and what immediately caught my
eye was a photo of a small Iraqi boy lying on a hospital bed with one

of his legs removed. The picture was accompanied by a poem written by a poet named Inquilab.

When translated to English, the poem reads like this:

"There are no singing birds in the sky
and on the date palm trees that gently kiss the heaven.

Your lies have poured smoke and fire globs.
Injuries don't check a child's age.

Heart full of shame!

Devil's mouth has sucked
oil and blood from the desert.
This drop of ink and the curse won't ever stop,
and will cure the wounds.

The arrows of Native Americans,
The muscles of black men,
The flags of Vietnam,
And the storms of the deserts,
Will someday grow and stand tall
midst the cracks of your White House."

I felt a chill as I read this poem.

I had spent most of my childhood in that little colonial hill country town before migrating to America. I knew the sentiments of the people who lived there. Most of them were extremely poor and had no time to think about the local politics that went on around them, let alone the rest of the world. Occasionally they watched Hollywood movies and thought Americans were the most superior human beings in the whole world. And yet now I had received a magazine containing a powerful poem about the war in Iraq, a poem which cursed the Americans. And the majority of those who live in that little town and read this publication are not Muslims.

A year later, I traveled to Sri Lanka to visit my parents, who were spending some time in our old town, and I met an interesting man whom I'll call Ahmed. (His name has been changed to protect his privacy.)

Ahmed was my driver for the few days that I traveled around the town to visit friends and relatives. He belonged to the tiny Muslim community of the town; the majority of inhabitants are either Buddhists or Hindus.

He was very prompt, polite, and always displayed that pleasant humility one finds among Sri Lankans—when they are not fighting among each other.

Muslims in Sri Lanka are the only community that largely avoided the two decade civil war that has killed more than 60,000 people. They were caught between the two fighting elements—the government, and the rebels known as Tamil Tigers—and always maintained a fair neutrality during the conflict. The Muslims who lived in my town were very peaceful. They never demonstrated any type of extremism or violence, and largely got along very well with other communities.

One day, on our way to my friend's house, as we drove through the rough and dangerous roads of my hilly old town, Ahmed slowly and politely started a conversation.

"Sir, do you mind if I ask you something?"

"No. Of course not, Ahmed. What is it?" I replied with surprise.

"Do you like America?" he asked.

"Of course. Yes. I like it immensely, except for the fact that I miss my parents. Why do you ask?"

"What's wrong with Bush? Why is he behaving like this? Why did you all elect him again?"

I was caught by surprise. Ten years ago, I couldn't even have imagined a person in my town discussing world politics, let alone naming the American president. Only the two or three percent who considered themselves intellectuals ever talked of world affairs, and even then only after two solid gulps of local alcohol.

Before answering Ahmed, I asked him a question.

"Ahmed, do you hate Americans?"

"Sir, to be honest, I think I do."

I was shaken. I didn't expect this from him.

"Can I ask you why?"

"Look what they have done to Iraq. More than 300,000 have died. What did Americans gain?"

Ahmed was no longer polite in his questioning.

"Ahmed, can I ask you a couple of questions before answering you?"

"Yes, sir, please!" He had resumed his humility.

"Ahmed, look, I know it's not easy for me to convince you. Not all Americans support the war in Iraq. Do you know how many voted against President Bush? Even those who voted for him did so for many other domestic reasons. It's not fair to hate Americans for the mistakes their government made. There are a lot of good things about America. You may think I like America for the money and luxury that I enjoy out there. Partially, yes. But there are other reasons, too."

I could see I had Ahmed's attention. I continued, "Let me ask you this: What would happen if you drew a picture of a Sri Lankan president as a chimpanzee and stuck it on the bumper of your mini-van?"

Ahmed looked at me with slight surprise and smiled. "I would be abducted in a white mini-van, and you would probably find me dead in a river," said Ahmed.

"See, that's the difference. Do you know how many cartoons were published in America comparing President Bush to a monkey?

Nobody will ever kill those who draw them and nobody could ever abduct them in a white van. That's how American democracy works," I said politely.

"Really? Did they really draw pictures of Bush like a monkey?" Ahmed was indeed amazed.

"Let me ask you another question, Ahmed. How many local radio stations or newspapers broadcast or write commentaries about minorities and the issues they face in government controlled areas of Sri Lanka?"

Ahmed raised his eyebrows and whispered, "Sir, do you know our prime minister tried to kill a famous businessman who owns a couple of TV stations for opposing his party?"

"I read about it somewhere."

"Also, sir, a couple of journalists were killed for writing commentaries supporting the rebels. And the rebels won't let anyone go against their interests either. They expect all minorities to support them. This place is a mess." I could hear the frustration in Ahmed's voice.

"See," I said, "in America, there are hundreds of radio and TV stations that both support and oppose the government. People can write whatever they want and say whatever they want. Nobody gets killed for writing or saying something. It's called freedom of speech. That's something you have not heard of."

Ahmed nodded and looked at the mountain range that appeared far away.

"Tell me, Ahmed, is it fair to hate Americans for the crimes and mistakes their government makes?" I asked him politely.

"Maybe not! But I'm still not convinced. There is something that bothers me, sir. I think you feel better there, so it's natural that you like them."

"Ahmed, it may be hard for you to believe, but there have been many occasions when I have really felt proud to be in America. Not that I think everything Americans do is right. But there is a lot more to America than most people think. In my opinion, the only problem in America is that the media has repeatedly failed to tell Americans what the rest of the world thinks about them. Here is a classic example: You have very strong feelings about Americans. You live in a tiny unknown town on a very small island that many Americans can't even locate on a world map. There is very little the media does to showcase your opinion to the public. The only time they showed Sri Lanka on American television was when the tsunami hit. You know something, people in my company donated more than $50,000 for the victims. And a company called Amazon, which sells books on the Internet, collected more than $15 million within two days from its customers. That should tell you something, don't you think?"

I was trying my best to tell him the reality.

"Sir, do you know none of those donations reached the victims? There were some hawks within our government who didn't let the money go to hard-hit areas in the north and east to reach the minorities, and neither the American government nor their embassies here did anything. They were either busy killing people in Iraq or worried about something else. Even Bill Clinton, who visited here after the tsunami, was not allowed to visit some areas, and he just didn't bother to question the fact. I think if Sri Lanka had oil, the approach would have been different."

"What can American people do about that Ahmed? They can only do what they can: give money. And they gave generously."

"That's true," he replied with a nod.

Ahmed's thin, humble face told me a lot more than what his lips whispered. He will never be convinced. He thinks all Americans are brutal killers. But at least I tried. I tried to make him think. For the rest of the journey, Ahmed told me about his family and how hard life has been for him.

I left Sri Lanka within a week, and my hectic New Jersey life slowly started to consume me as usual. But something repeatedly bothered me: The lingering look of frustration and doubt in Ah-med's eyes.

How many Ahmeds are out there in this restless world? Do Americans know what a poor, modest driver in a remote town in Sri Lanka, a country which has repeatedly shown pro-Western bias, thinks about them? Should Americans care? Will they care?

Then the writer in me conceived something interesting. What if I tried to collect and publish these rare and unknown world opinions? There may be millions of them. What to pick? Where to pick? Will Americans read them?

Ahmed's question echoed in my mind.

"Why did Americans re-elect Bush?"

The question was intriguing. My mission began.

I contacted all of my friends around the world and asked them to send every op-ed and cartoon that was published during President Bush's re-election. I thought the 2004 election was the time the whole world came together to write about Americans. November 2004 was when the whole world collectively expelled their thoughts about America through mouth, pens, and pencils. Bush's re-election was the event on which to focus. These opinions are pertinent forever and can be used to carefully decrypt the world mindset every time we think about the rest of the world in the future.

Friends volunteered. So did Google and its useful translation feature. I took a week off from my programming job and Googled every single article that was published in every tiny part of the globe during the 2004 U.S. elections.

I was very particular about finding articles from the lesser known parts of the world, and I largely avoided English-speaking countries such as England, Australia, New Zealand, and most other Western countries that our media had access to. I assumed most of us would either have read these articles or would not care about them. It was not an easy task. But I was overwhelmed by the content. I was able to find editorials, opinions, cartoons, and caricatures from forty different countries, including one from Vanuatu, the tiny little Pacific island off of Papua New Guinea that became famous because of the television show *Survivor*.

It took me a couple of months to sort through them to find the right ones and to avoid monotony and overlaps. It took me almost a year to contact the publishers to obtain reprint permissions. Nevertheless, the effort was worth it. When I finally compiled the articles and cartoons to create this small yet important book, I was thrilled. I knew I had produced a worthy read. I felt relieved.

Ahmed's humble face appeared in front of me again.

I'm letting the American people know what you think about them, my friend. I'm also letting them know what millions of Ahmeds from around the world think about Americans at this very important juncture in world history. Let them read it, and I'll let you know about the responses next time I visit you.

I then realized something that hadn't occurred to me until I finished this book. Modern immigrants like me can play a very positive and instrumental role in bringing America one step closer to the rest of the world, hence making global peace a possibility. This may an unspoken duty every modern immigrant owes to America and the rest of the world.

It has been two years since President Bush was re-elected, and things have changed a lot since then. People who voted last time around may be able to employ this book to examine how the world has progressed in the last two years. In addition, this book contains some very interesting facts about how American voters choose their politicians. For example, an interesting opinion written by Tom Gross from Israel analyzes how Jews in America vote. Another opinion from the Caribbean analyzes how the ever-increasing Caribbean immigrant population should be voting in the future.

The book contains eight chapters. The first chapter explores articles that were written prior to the election. The second chapter covers the immediate reaction to President Bush's re-election. I inserted two lighter sections (chapter three and four) to make this book a little entertaining. (Did Democrats consider migrating to Canada? Did Osama bin Laden help Bush win the second term?)

The fifth chapter is about the Jewish and Israeli reaction to President Bush's re-election, which I thought was vital if this book was to be balanced. The sixth chapter is about what the world thought of the faith-based approach of President Bush. I also included a separate chapter to analyze how the world looked at the negative side of John Kerry. And the final chapter takes an optimistic look at the future. I concluded the book with a very personal note that I couldn't resist inserting. The content of my conclusion is extremely close to my heart and I take it very seriously.

I hope you all will enjoy and appreciate the effort.

Happy and thoughtful reading!

Acknowledgements

T his book wouldn't have been a possibility without the generous support and help of the following publishers and authors who wholeheartedly allowed me to reprint their creations. I owe the success of this book to the following people, and thank them a thousand times over.

♣ Stavro Jabra, the famous cartoonist of Beirut, Lebanon, for granting permission to publish his work that made the stunning cover page possible.

♣ Waheed Odusile of Nigeria and the publishers of *Nigerian Sun News*.

♣ Nadia Al-Sakkaf of *The Yemen Times*, Yemen.

♣ Patrick Chappatte the cartoonist of Geneva daily *Le Temps* and the *International Herald Tribune*.

♣ Jonathan Rosenblum and the publishers of *Maariv International* and *Jerusalem Post*, Israel.

♣ Tom Gross and the publishers of *Israel Insider*, Israel.

♣ Harold Pinter, 2005 Nobel laureate for literature, and the staff of the Nobel Foundation, Stockholm, Sweden: Jonna Petter son, Lorenette Gozzo, and Annika Pontikis.

♣ I.K. Gyasi of Ghana and J. Ato Kobbie, the editor of *Ghanian Chronicle*.

- ♣ Julius Hansen, the cartoonist of *Horsens Folkeblad*, Denmark.

- ♣ Patrick Corrigan, the cartoonist of *The Toronto Star*, Canada.

- ♣ Dr Farrukh Saleem of Islamabad, Pakistan.

- ♣ Faris Sanabani of the *Yemen Observer*, Yemen.

- ♣ Professor Vinay Lal of UCLA, CA.

- ♣ GADO, the political cartoonist from Kenya.

- ♣ Zafar Sobhan and the publishers of *Daily Star* of Bangladesh.

- ♣ Steve Nease of Oakville, Canada.

- ♣ Patrick Seale and Ayad Tassabehji — the publisher of *Daily Star*, Lebanon.

- ♣ Khaled Almaeena, the publisher of *Arab News*, Saudi Arabia.

- ♣ The editors of *Cairo Press Review*, Egypt.

- ♣ Barbara Gloudon and the publishers of *Jamaica Observer*, Jamaica.

- ♣ Timothy Bancroft-Hinchey and the publishers of *Pravda Online*, Russia.

- ♣ Jonathan Shapiro of Cape Town, South Africa.

- ♣ Anthony Capron and the publishers of *Nassau Guardian*, Bahamas.

- ♣ The publishers of *Manila Bulletin*, Philippines.

- ♣ The publishers of *Accra Mail*, Ghana.

- ♣ Keeble McFarlene and the publishers of *Jamaica Observer*, Jamaica.

- ♣ The publishers of *Port Villa Presse*, Vanuatu.

- ♣ The publishers of *The Onion*.

- ♣ Gwynne Dyer and the publishers of *Trinidad and Tobago Express*.

- ♣ Jovial Rantao and the publishers of *The Sunday Independent*, South-Africa.

- ♣ Hasan Bleibel of *Al-Mustakbal*, Beirut, Lebanon.

- ♣ Tarik Atia of *Cairolive.com*, Egypt.

- ♣ VAL, of *VIETBAO*, Vietnam.

- ♣ Donato and the publishers of *Toronto Sun*, Canada.

- ♣ Sen. Edgardo Angara, Philippines.

- ♣ Munodii Kunzwa and the publishers of *Daily News* Harare, Zimbabwe.

- ♣ Publishers of *Jordan Times*, Jordan.

♣ Publishers of *Digital Chosun*, South Korea.

♣ Publishers of *The Star*, South Africa.

♣ Daniel S. Hamilton and Joseph P. Quinlan and the publishers of *International Herald Tribune*.

♣ Publishers of *Nandalala*, Sri Lanka.

♣ Dr. James J. Zogby, President of Arab American Institute in Washington, DC.

♣ Frank Boyle of *Edinburgh Evening Times*, Scotland and Martyn Turner of *The Irish Times*, Ireland.

♣ Christo Komarnitski of Sofia, Bulgaria.

♣ Special thanks to Dr. Piyush Mathur of Virginia Tech, Melvin Durai(author and humor columnist) of Winnipeg, Canada, Joanne Starer of ReadLine Editorial Services, Skylar Burris(editor of *Ancient Path* Literary Magazine) and the editorial and marketing staff of Midpoint Trade Books for providing editorial guidance.

CHAPTER ONE

Great Expectations

*W*hen I started the long process of gathering the opinion pieces, two "open letters" caught my attention. The first letter, written by the Nigerian columnist Waheed Odusile, appeared in the* Nigerian Sun News. *The second, by Timothy Bancroft-Hinchey, was published by* Pravda Online, *the website of a very popular newspaper from Russia.*

Odusile's powerful, thought-provoking, and intriguing letter, published in what's considered a moderate Islamic country, gives us a glimpse into what the rest of the world was expecting from American voters prior to the election.

It was not an easy task to find Waheed. I sent numerous emails to him and to his publisher, The Nigerian Sun News, *and waited for many weeks. There was no reply. I woke up early one morning and sent a reminder, and Waheed replied immediately.*

"With all pleasure. Go ahead!"

Letter to Americans

By Waheed Odusile
Monday, October 25, 2004

Dear Yankees, Fraternal greetings to you all. As you prepare to elect another president and some members of Congress on Tuesday, 2nd November, kindly spare a thought for the rest of the world, especially the non-Americans scattered around the world, who are in love with your country's democracy.

You might not believe it but it is true. Anytime there was going to be an election in your country, either the midterm congressional election or the four yearly presidential polls, the rest of the world virtually moves into frenzy as we eagerly await the result at the end of polling. Here in Nigeria on polling day, the Public Affairs section of your embassy often extends invitation to the media and some friends of the United States to come and witness live, albeit on television, the voting process, announcement of the result, acceptance speech by the victor and loser conceding victory, and post election analysis.

The high point of the night is a mock voting by those present. And you know what, since I've been attending here in Lagos, the Democrats have been winning. The reason is not far fetched; the Republicans are not loved at all here. They are seen as hardliners who think little of others.

Their interest is money, money, money and power. They care less about others.

As with the Democrats, though they too always put America first, they don't ride the rest of the world roughshod, and at least, they still put an appearance of human face to everything they do, in relation to the rest of the world. That's the perception of the majority here. You need to see how disappointed most Nigerians were the last time you voted for a president. I am talking about the 2000 election that brought President George W. Bush to power.

Our belief is that he stole the Presidency from then Vice President Al Gore, the Democratic Party candidate. To use the common Nigerian phrase for such victory, I would say he rigged the election. The outcome of that 2000 election has increased the number of Nigerians now interested in elections in your country. You would be surprised to learn that if your up coming elections were to be opened to Nigerians, more Nigerians would turn out to vote than the number that turned out in our 2003 presidential election. By the way, the result of that election (2003) that brought President Olusegun Obasanjo to power is still being contested in court some 18 months after the victor had taken office and the loser had still not congratulate his 'victorious' opponent. Can you imagine that? Our court here had still not disposed off that case. I wonder what the reaction would be if this were to happen in the U.S.

In fact one of the attractions of your country's democracy to us was the way and manner your Supreme Court and the lower courts, handled swiftly, Gore's challenge to Bush's victory. Though while we disagreed with the outcome, we nonetheless salute the system for coming up with a decision on time before the inauguration. We were equally happy at the way Gore conceded victory in spite of the fact that he won the popular vote and the glaring disenfranchisement of his supporters in Florida, Miami Dade County in particular. We saw it as a victory for your democracy and something from which we can learn.

Our fears way back in 2000 were that a former Governor of Texas, lacking in experience especially about world affairs and without human compassion, being entrusted with the most powerful office in the world could be dangerous not only to you Americans, but the rest of humanity. I am sure if you ask yourself this question, whether your country and indeed the rest of the world have been a better place since Bush came to power, and you are sincere enough with an honest answer, you will answer in the negative. President Bush since he took office, especially since after 9/11, has made himself and America, more enemies in the world than he inherited from President Bill Clinton. Many see him as one if not the most dangerous person in the world today. You know why? People here as well as elsewhere outside the US regard him and his neocons colleagues, as a bunch of arrogant, gun totting cowboys and pseudo-religious bigots who see nothing good or sensible in what others are doing or think.

We were all shocked by the event of 9/11. You would be surprised at the depth of hatred Nigerians had for Osama bin Laden and his al Qeda group of terrorists after the famous Twin Towers and part of Pentagon were destroyed. And if bin Laden were to be living in Nigeria as he's believed to be in the border between Pakistan and Afghanistan he would have been handed over to your C.I.A that time. That was a measure of our support for America that time. But unfortunately, I don't think that is still the situation here today. You wonder what happened. Your president George Bush, has within three years squandered all the sympathies and goodwill the events of 9/11 generated for your country around the world including here in Nigeria. How? Well so many reasons. But I think the major one is the Iraq war. Many here believe that war was uncalled for. It was a revenge war to avenge the loss of Bush senior's Presidency to Bill Clinton in 1992. It was clear that the first Gulf war cost Bush senior a second presidential term. So the removal of Iraqi leader Saddam Hussein under whatever pretence, was a programme of Bush junior's White House right from the first day, 9/11 only provided an excuse.

If you recollect, hardly was any voice raised against your country' armed invasion of Afghanistan to topple the Taliban regime that was harboring bin Laden. With or without a United Nations backing, almost all believed that action was justified under the doctrine of self defense. But this was not so with the invasion of Iraq and the overthrow of Saddam Hussein. To compound the situation, Bush and his fellow travelers in his so called coalition of the willing, especially Prime Minister Tony Blair of Britain lied to us, the UN in particular, to justify their heinous crime in Iraq. We had always suspected they were lying but they succeeded in hoodwinking us with their cooked up evidence of Saddam's Weapons of Mass Destruction, the destruction of which they said was the motive behind their rabid desire to oust Hussein. Now our fears have been confirmed. Saddam had nothing but bravado.

Bush knew or knows nothing about the job he sought in 2000 and which was given to him; he only surrounds himself with war mongers like Donald Rumsfield and Dick Cheney. People who have no qualms even if innocent lives are to be lost in the pursuit of their neo-conservative ideas.

Bush was in Africa the other day and honestly I can't remember what he came here to do. He was even in Nigeria. But I am sure if you ask people around the African continent most will be able to vividly recall the visits of former President Bill Clinton to Africa. Even after leaving the White House, the man from Little Rock Arkansas is still very popular not only in Africa, but other parts of the world.

I understand you Yankees still love him. You know why he is loved here? He has a human touch to everything. While in office, he did not use the power and might of America just anyhow, as Bush is doing now. When he acted in the interest of America, the whole world understood. He wasn't carried away by the sole super power status of America. He was a humble president even with his enormous powers and the world respected him for that, and he earned respect for America and Americans around the world. Not so with Bush. He is about the most hated American leader around the world in recent memory.

Can you imagine at a recent meeting of past Nobel Prize winners in Barcelona Spain, the laureates, except the Americans in attendance, signed a document urging you people to vote out Bush on November 2nd? I don't know whether that letter has been made public by the media in the U.S. You see, that is the general position around the world. In fact that is why I am writing this letter to you. Please make the world a saver place by voting out George Bush on November 2nd and you will be doing your country and the rest of humanity a lot of good.

By the way I read that the Boston Redsox defied the odds and won 4-3 from the best of seven series against their bitter rival (can't remember the name now) from I think New York, to become the first team in the U.S to win and qualify for the world series after being 3 games down. What a feat. I also understand Senator John Kerry, the Democratic Party candidate in the November 2nd election is a Redsox fan. Does that say anything about the up coming election?"

Patrick Chappatte, Cartoons on World Affairs. Patrick's cartoons appear in the Geneva daily *Le Temps* and in the Sunday edition of the *Neue Zurcher Zeitung*. He also does a weekly cartoon for the *International Herald Tribune*.

Never in the History

The following letter was published by Pravda Online, *from Russia. While researching* Pravda *to get the permission for this column (which they wholeheartedly grant to everyone, provided due credit is given), I found an interesting piece that described the history of this publication.*

According to Pravda Online, *the original newspaper* Pravda *from 1912 until 1991 was a publication of the Communist Party, and, as such, it became a state-owned newspaper.*

In 1991, when the Soviet Union collapsed, the newspaper was shut down and was re-launched after few years of struggle. Due to a difference of opinion, a group of journalists launched Pravda Online *in January of 1999, the first Russian newspaper of its kind.*

In spite of the fact that the journalists of both these publications are still in touch with each other, they have different conceptions about news. The newspaper Pravda *analyzes events from the point of view of the Communist Party's interests, whereas* Pravda Online *takes a pro-Russian approach to forming its policy.*

The following piece is from Pravda Online.

Never in the history of humankind has an election had so much at stake.
Timothy-Bancroft-Hinchey
www.pravda.ru

Dear friends,
As a journalist who has the good fortune to write for an international journal with millions of readers around the world, I have the individual responsibility to inform you of the feeling in the international

community regarding the outcome of the election on November 2nd.

As citizens of the United States of America, who have the power to endorse or to dismiss the policies of the Bush regime, you have a collective responsibility not only unto yourselves, but to the world, which will hold you accountable for your decision.

I write this letter as a citizen of this international community and as a journalist for a newspaper whose name is Pravda (Truth), I have the obligation to tell the truth, the whole truth and nothing but the truth.

I can say for a start that the vast majority of the international community will agree with the thoughts and requests expressed in this open letter. As proof, one only has to see the opinion polls held around the world, in which only a small handful of citizens from a tiny percentage of states prefer a re-election of George Bush to regime change in Washington.

It is not for foreigners to dictate to the people of the United States of America how to vote, however since the media in the USA is controlled and since people do not have access to the current of opinion in the international community, it is an act of friendship to inform the citizens of the USA how the world feels about the state of affairs today and it is our right as citizens of the world to express our concern, for the Bush administration that does not confine itself to its shores.

9/11 was a horrific event, which went against the grain of human civilization, as did the horrendous terrorist attack in the school of Beslan in the Russian Federation. However terrible these events were, it is necessary to envisage the facts with maturity and to draw the correct conclusions from them, not to use an evil event to justify another act of evil.

Unfortunately this is what the Bush regime has done. While the attack against Afghanistan was understandable in the circumstances (although such an attack had been planned well before 9/11, not because of the Taleban regime, which George Bush Senior created, but because of the gas pipeline from Turkmenistan to Pakistan), the attack against Iraq had nothing whatsoever to do with international terrorism.

From a moral point of view, the Bush regime could not have descended lower. Lies, forgery, blackmail, bullying and belligerence became the modus operandi of American diplomacy, instead of discussion, dialogue and debate, the fundamentals of democracy, which Bush and his clique of corporate elitists threw out of the window in their haste to get their hands on the resources of Iraq, a country which did not possess chemical or nuclear or biological weapons, despite the repeated claims that it did.

The raw truth is that Saddam Hussein was the man telling the truth and that George Bush was the one who "stiffed the world". The fundamental precepts which justified the war have since been refuted and denied, in their entirety, by the very people who stood before the cameras and lied through their teeth, saying they knew where the WMD were hidden and they knew where the evidence would be found.

These people are the members of the Bush regime, not one or two members, but all of them. It is not only George Bush who stands for election on November 2nd – it is the entire regime, including the substantially important Jewish lobby within Washington. It is not only Capitol Hill which controls your foreign policy, it is also, and with increasing importance, the Knesset in Tel Aviv.

George Bush may have tried his level best at being President of the United States of America and nobody doubts that he will have wanted to give it his best shot and do a good job. However, his background, his speeches and his skills, make it only too apparent that he does not have what it takes. Like the Texas he was born in, he is a Lone Ranger.

George Bush and his government have managed to divorce Washington from the international community. He dare not step off an aircraft in most countries and even in the home of his closest ally, the UK, he was the only visiting Head of State to have to run out of Number 10 Downing Street by the back door, because he was too scared to leave by the front, given the fury of the demonstrators against him.

Is this the image you wish to vote for on November 2nd?

George Bush and his administration spent four long years breaking every fibre of decency and each and every norm in practice in the diplomatic community. If New York is host to the United Nations Organization, how can it be justified to breach the UN Charter by attacking Iraq outside the auspices of this organization? Each and every resolution bears the express condition that any act of war must be the result of a separate resolution of the UN Security Council.

If Washington and London did not believe this to be the case, why did the USA and UK spend so many energies trying to secure the vote, only to deride this organism when they saw they could not win the day by diplomatic means? Hence the phrase, echoing around the international community: US out of UN or UN out of US.

George Bush has turned the USA into a pariah state in the international community and before the eyes of the citizens of the world.

The legacy of George Bush is unfortunately abject failure in everything he has done. Internally, it is up to the citizens of the USA to decide whether he has delivered on jobs, health care, welfare, pensions and so on – for this is nobody else's business. Externally, however, he has wholly destabilized a delicate region which he was advised not to enter.

Afghanistan is far from pacified, the Taleban are as strong as ever, the difference being now that the heroin trade has restarted. Fantastic for the cities of Russia and Europe, now flooded once more by prime quality smack. We can thank George Bush for that every time an old lady is kicked to death for her pension money by some guy who needs a fix.

Iraq was never a bastion of terrorism, as Rumsfeld now admits. It is now, only after the illegal, incompetent, unfounded invasion launched by George Bush. Cities like Fallujah, more than one year on, are still in the hands of Iraq's freedom fighters and now, the calls for British troops to help the US forces, who are losing control in Baghdad, are causing a political furore in London, due to the fact that the actions of the US armed forces would be considered war crimes in Europe.

The torture at Abu Ghraib was one symptom of a disease called George Bush and his neo-conservative, extremist, elitist regime, basically a group of super rich kids who thought nothing of spending two hundred thousand million dollars of your hard-earned money, which, you'd better believe it, you will pay a heavy price for in the coming years. Elect Bush again, and there will be more, much more.

You, the electors, will be the ones who pay, not Bush or Cheney or Rice or Rumsfeld or Wolfowitz. They've already filled their coffers, they only care about you before November 2nd. After that, all you can do is to sit back and watch as the horror unfolds before your eyes.

The final twist to this sordid and horrible tale is that the war crimes committed by the Pentagon have created a sullen hatred in the hearts and minds of the international community. The shock and awe we feel at learning how cluster bombs were dropped in civilian areas, for children to pick up thinking they were sweets, only to have their eyes and faces and futures and lives blown away, makes us stand together making a solemn and heartfelt request to our friends, or those we wish to count as friends, over the other side of the Atlantic.

Please, consider very carefully what you are doing on November 2nd. We want to have the USA back among us as part of the international community of nations. A vote for Bush is a vote for more wars, more terrorism, more violence, a shift further away from the welcoming arms of the community of nations, which wants to live together as brothers, not in hatred.

Killing tens of thousands of civilians is not Christian, it is evil and the callousness with which this issue is faced by the Bush regime is witness to the coldness in their hearts and minds, a coldness which creates shock and revulsion in the community of nations. In Europe, in Africa, in Asia, in Latin America, in Canada.

If you cannot bring yourselves to vote for any of the other contestants, then at least, please, consider not voting for Bush. In a nutshell, there are no two ways about it. Killing tens of thousands of civilians by strafing their homes, mutilating tens of thousands more, committing rape and torture on a scale unseen outside the concentration camps of Hitler, amounts to war crimes, murder.

Voting for Bush is voting for a war criminal and a mass murderer.

In the name of the world community,
For the Love of God,
Timothy.
Respectfully and in friendship.

3/11 2004   No text.

Julius Hansen, Horsens Folkeblad, Denmark.

Bush: A Study in Failure

The following opinion was written by a well known African journalist I.K Gyasi from Ghana - Former UN Secretary General Kofi Annan's country.

The piece appeared in the Ghanaian Chronicle, *the largest independent daily newspaper published in Ghana.*

Bush: A study in failure
I. K. Gyasi
Monday, May 24, 2004

When a new history of the United States of America comes to be written, the narrative will show that the biggest disaster that ever happened to that country was President George W. Bush Jnr., and not the calamity of September 11, 2001.

And if George Bush should write his memoirs after being voted out of the White House, he should title the work, "Failure" with the sub-title, "How the Son Never Rose."

George Bush is the clearest example of how, in spite of all the privileges and advantages at one's disposal, one can easily fail to succeed in life.

George Bush will never be in the same league as George Washington, Abraham Lincoln, Frank Delano Roosevelt, J. F. Kennedy, Jimmy Carter, Dwight D. Eisenhower and Bill Clinton, for example.

While George W. Bush Snr., (the father) was carving a niche for himself in American society as ambassador, Director of the Central Intelligence Agency (CIA) and later as president of the United States, what was his son doing?

He was leading the life of the typical wastrel: dissipation and total aimlessness in life. In fact, as everyone knows, he had to be rescued from that life and rehabilitated by a group of Wesleyan priests. One wonders whether the rehabilitation was one hundred percent successful.

This is the man who became the President of the United States of America under extremely dubious circumstances. In deed, if the way Bush was "elected" had happened in a so-called Third World or developing country, the "civilized and democratic" people of the Western world, would have cried "Foul."

The Florida vote was crucial. And Florida was where the elder brother of Bush was the Governor. Some ballot boxes disappeared for a time. Barriers were erected to stop some Black Americans from going to exercise their right to vote. They are known to vote for the Democratic Party.

A faulty voting machine was used that resulted in the votes of several Black Americans being rendered invalid.

The Democratic candidate for the Presidency, Al Gore, insisted on manual recounting of the votes. As the recounts threatened to turn the vote in Al Gore's favour, the matter ended up at the United States Federal Supreme Court.

There, with seven out of the nine Justices of the court being Republicans put on the Court mainly by previous Republican Presidents, the verdict unsurprisingly went in favour of Bush. Al Gore accepted the verdict with grace.

At the inauguration of a President of the United States, a number played is titled, "Hail To The Chief."

Having "won" the election under such unconvincing and highly questionable circumstances, it is no wonder that some of the spectators shouted, 'Hail To The Thief." Sure, he had stolen the Presidency, no doubt about that, Probably realizing his debilitating shortcomings as a person and as "a cut-purse president" George W. Bush set out to terrorize the rest of the world.

With a deadpan face, eyes almost shut out by his eyelids, snakelike lips, hectoring speeches and a bellicose posture, Bush sought to create the impression that he was the modern-day equivalent of the Old Wild West Sheriff who, alone or in the company of a posse, rides out of town to catch the bad guy and bring him to Justice.

On the contrary, Bush has proved himself rather the bad guy who, with his sidekicks, rides into town, pulls out his Smith & Wesson or Colt 45 pistols, heads for the nearest saloon, and starts to cower everyone by indiscriminating firing into the ceiling.

Came September 11 and Bush must have thought that a wonderful opportunity had been presented to him to embark on a crusade to rid the world of all the bad guys whom he describes as terrorists.

Buoyed up by his invasion of Afghanistan and the driving away of the Taliban regime, Bush must have convinced himself that he was invincible.

He must have been convinced further by the people he had assembled around him: Dick Cheney, his Vice President; Collin Powell, his Secretary of State; Donald Rumsfeld, his Secretary for Defense; Ms Condoleesa Rice, his national security Advisor, and John Ashcroft, his Attorney-General.

These people, as shown by the Guinness Book of Records, are all billionaires. The god they worship is an insatiable appetite for wealth, power and world domination.

Casting their eyes around, they saw what Bush came to describe as countries that terrorized the rest of the world through state-sponsored destabilization of other countries.

To Bush, these countries, namely Iraq, Iran and North Korea, formed an "axis of evil" that had to be destroyed. Attacked them one after the other and such so-called "rogue states" like Libya and Syria would quickly mend their ways.

The conquest of Iraq and the removal of Saddam Hussein would open up that country for economic rape. Most of the people around him had made their fortunes in oil, especially Dick Cheney and Condoleesa Rice. The oil fields of Iraq were there for the picking.

Why not attack Saddam Hussein on the false pretext that, contrary to the resolutions of the United States, he had acquired, or was seriously acquiring, weapons of mass destruction, namely chemical, biological and nuclear weapons (WMDs)?

Without the sanction of a resolution by the United Nations, George Bush, the World's Number One Policeman or Sheriff, wore his ten-gallon hat and his cow boy boots, buckled his belt with two holsters for his fighting guns, swung into the saddle, and headed straight for Iraq. Dear readers, you know the rest of the story of the invasion of Iraq and its aftermath.

In Afghanistan, Osama bin Laden, fingered as the villain who masterminded the September 11 catastrophe, reportedly remains at large. So are the leaders of the Taliban regime.

Thanks to the power and the lure of money, Saddam Hussein has been betrayed to Bush. Far from Saddam's capture and the disbanding of his army ending hostilities in Iraq, Bush continues to sink in the Iraqi quicksand.

Far from being the Liberator bringing peace, development and prosperity, Bush has only succeeded in introducing chaos, needless bloodshed and disintegration to that country.

When he allegedly visited American soldiers in Iraq, he could only do so "Nicodemously," instead of riding in an open vehicle to acknowledge the cheers of a grateful people.

It is said that he wore a military uniform, ostensibly to empathize with the troops but more likely to hide his real identity so that he did not become a target. The man "highlighted it" out of town as fast as he had entered it.

On June 30, 2004, Bush will hand over the house of cards he has built in Iraq to a group. He knows very well that that house will collapse but it is anything to get out of that hellhole.

American jingoism, the policy of "my country right or wrong" and her hypocrisy and double standards pre-date the Bush Presidency.

Still, there can be no doubt that Bush in his almost four years in office has adopted the crudest type of foreign policy that has raised this American character to record heights.

The shocking record of the treatment of prisoners in Iraq and at the Guantanamo Base in Cuba has shown the ugliest face of George Bush and his America.

Today, the worst type of a so-called Third World dictator is an angel compared to George Bush. No wonder that 50 (fifty) former American diplomats have written to warn him about the effect of his policies. According to them, such policies are losing friends for America.

Today, George Bush encourages Israel to disregard international law, respect for human rights and to carry out acts of genocide. At least other American Presidents tried to bring about peace between the Israelis and the Palestinians.

Today, George Bush says that thc prisoncrs at the Guantanamo base are not regular prisoners of war but "illegal combatants." They are also said not to be on United States soil so the laws of the United States do not apply to them. Consequently, Bush has the right to hold them forever at the Base and under constant torture.

Far from winning his so-called war on terror, George Bush rather continues to stoke up the fires that forge terrorists around the world.

George W. Bush, this "king of shreds and patches" (apologies to Shakespeare's Hamlet), has become the biggest terrorist of all time.

He has succeeded in reducing America to the lowest point or nadir of her history while he himself has sunk lower than a snake's belly.

This is the man who wants another stay in the White House.

Who will save US from Homegrown Extremists?

Dr Farrukh Saleem is an Islamabad, Pakistan-based freelance columnist. He wrote this analytical column for The News *which is published by the* Jang Group, *the largest English and Urdu publication group in Pakistan. This opinion was published few months prior to the election.*

Who Will Save U.S. from Homegrown Extremists?
Dr Farrukh Saleem, Islamabad, Pakistan.

J Leon Holmes wrote that "wives must be subordinate to their husbands". Holmes also believes that there was no difference between "abortion rights activists and Nazis". President George W Bush nominated Holmes to become a US District Judge.

Jay S Bybee, in a memo to the Justice Department, justified the "use of torture as an interrogation technique". President George W Bush nominated Jay S Bybee to become a Circuit Judge, United States Court of Appeals for the Ninth Circuit.

Dick Cheney has grown into a true radical, a genuine Superhawk. Cheney's influence on the younger Bush has furthered an already extremist agenda. Cheney continues to insist that Iraq has Weapons of Mass Destruction and that Saddam and Osama are linked. Cheney supports a "never-ending war against radical Islam". Dick Cheney is President George W Bush's vice.

John Ashcroft has long been a favourite of Christian Rightists. Ashcroft supports the use of secret military tribunals. Ashcroft firmly believes in the government's right "to take people away and lock them up without anyone knowing exactly who or precisely why". President George W Bush made Ashcroft the Attorney

General of the United States, the head of the Department of Justice and the chief law enforcement officer of the Federal Government.

Paul Wolfowitz has to be the truest of all true radicals. Wolfowitz always stood for unilateral pre-emptive action. Wolfowitz has always wanted to take on Iraq, Iran, North Korea, Syria and the rest of the world in order to "safeguard US interests, promote American values" and guarantee American "access to vital raw materials, primarily Persian Gulf oil.... (excerpts taken from the 'Defence Planning Guidance' authored by Paul Wolfowitz)." President George W Bush made Wolfowitz America's Deputy Defence Secretary (Rumsfeld had to be kept as a figurehead just because Wolfowitz was extremely controversial).

Karl Rove is a conservative, Catholic fundamentalist and a Republican to the extreme right. Rove managed to avoid the draft but now wants America to take on the "mullahs of Iran". Rove is often described as "Bush's Brain" or the president's inner conservative conscience. Rove's political, as well as his policy interests both revolve around Catholicism. Rove feels that "Iraq was only the beginning of the broader struggle against the 'terror masters'. Iran, Iraq, Syria and Saudi Arabia are the big four, and then there's Libya." The only people who spend more time with the president — than does Rove — are Cheney, Rice and the First Lady. James Moore, writing for The Los Angeles Times, stated: "Karl Rove led the nation to war to improve the political prospects of George W Bush. I know how surreal that sounds. But I also know it is true." Rove is President George W Bush's Senior Political Adviser.

Richard Perle had called for an immediate all-out war with the former Soviet Union. Perle has been the most inflexible of hardliners (for which he was dubbed the 'Prince of Darkness'). In 1996, Perle wrote a policy paper for Benjamin Netanyahu (Israel's PM from 1996 to 1999) mapping out "removal of Saddam Hussein and the installation of a Hashemite monarchy in Baghdad, which would serve as a first step towards eliminating the anti-Israeli governments of

35

Syria, Lebanon, Saudi Arabia, and Iran..." On 19 February 1998, Perle signed an 'Open Letter to the President' proposing "a comprehensive political and military strategy for bringing down Saddam and his regime (Clinton ignored it)." President George W Bush made Perle the Chairman of the Defence Policy Board (the Pentagon's advisory panel).

George W Bush, as per his personal testimony, is a 'Born Again through Jesus Christ'. For Bush, the 'war on terrorism' is his "evangelical vision of Good vs. Evil". Bush's simplicity in faith "inhibits self-examination and repentant action, critical components of any faith". Last year, Israeli PM Ariel Sharon, President George Bush and Palestinian PM Mahmoud Abbas met in Aqaba. According to PM Abbas, President Bush told them that, "God told me to strike at al Qaeda and I struck them, and then he instructed me to strike at Saddam, which I did...."

Bush claims to know everything about the dangerous spread of fundamentalism in other religions. It takes a fundamentalist to know a fundamentalist!

Ron Suskind writing for The New York Times argues that President Bush has created a "faith-based presidency" and that "the faith-based presidency is with-us-or-against-us model...."

Michael Kelly, a columnist for The Washington Post, wrote, "What President Bush aspires to now, is not exactly imperialism. It is something more like armed evangelism".

Holmes, Bybee, Cheney, Ashcroft, Wolfowitz, Rove and Perle play deaf to everyone who differs from their neo-conservative fundamentalist agenda. A Washington-insider recently quipped: "Bush [is] like a blind man in a room full of deaf people."

To be sure, Holmes, Bybee, Cheney, Ashcroft, Wolfowitz, Rove and Perle are unrepresentative of the US population. To be certain, Cheney, Ashcroft, Wolfowitz, Rove and Perle are also unrepresentative of America's mainstream foreign policy establishment.

The New York Times recently editorialised: "We have specific fears about what would happen in a second Bush term, particularly regarding the Supreme Court. The record so far gives us plenty of cause for worry (8 out of 9 Supreme Court justices are over 65 —the Chief Justice turned 80 — and a second Bush presidency may get a chance to appoint up to four new anti-choice, anti-privacy conservative judges, and that could change the way America decides issues for the following 30 years)."

The New York Times editorial continues, "There is no denying that this race is mainly about Mr Bush's disastrous tenure. Nearly four years ago, after the Supreme Court awarded him the presidency, Mr Bush came into office amid popular expectation that he would acknowledge his lack of a mandate by sticking close to the centre. Instead, he turned the government over to the radical right. Mr Bush installed John Ashcroft, a favourite of the far right with a history of insensitivity to civil liberties, as attorney general. Mr Bush's obsession with Saddam Hussein seemed closer to zealotry than mere policy...."

"Ministers of the evangelical movement," Newsweek pointed out, "form the core of the Republican Party, which controls all of the capital for the first time in a half century." Just who will stop the American radical right?

Who will save America from her home-grown extremists?

It is up to the Americans to Decide

The following reader comment was published in the Yemen Times *prior to the election.*

Yemen Times *and its editors were awarded the National Press Club's (NPC) International Award for Freedom of the Press for 1995. As the one of the few sources of current information on Yemen, the newspaper serves as a vital contact point for foreigners interested in Yemen. As its publisher and chief editor Professor Abdulaziz Al-Saqqaf says:*

"*We use the* Yemen Times *to make Yemen a good world citizen.*"

The editor of the Yemen Times, *Nadia Al-Sakkaf, was very prompt in replying to my emails and had no second thoughts about granting permission for the following reader comment and the editorial that appears afterwards.*

It is up to the Americans to Decide:
Yemen Times – Reader Comment
Mohamed Saeed

The fate of the warmonger and international terrorist, George Bush, is now in the hands of the American public. The American public has to decide whether they want Bush the warmonger to remain in office for another term and bring more destruction, misery and insecurity for them and the whole world. A recent research, conducted by global newspapers, confirmed that Bush and his policies receives only minority support and the world would prefer Kerry to be the next US president (witness 16/10/04).

Therefore it's important that the world mass media send reporters to America to cover the elections, as America is no more a democracy and a free country that it used to be. Bush's party controls the American media. Also the voting machines that are going to be used can easily be manipulated. This election is very important as it will determine the future of world peace and shape the future for generations to come. I hope the peace-loving people of America understand the fact that the world will not have real peace unless this terrorist and warmonger is voted out.

Patrick Corrigan, *The Toronto Star*, Canada

US Election Impacts us all
Yemen Times - Editorial
Nov 4th 2004

The US elections are now over. The winner was still unknown by the time we went to the press, but it is essential to note that whoever won, we are all affected.

Being the most influential country in the world, the USA has a say in the affairs of many other nations. Whether with its political influence, its economic contributions in international organizations, its massive consumption of energy, and other arenas, the USA is no doubt the single most dominant country in world affairs.

This means that the elections in the USA will define many policies throughout the world. This is why Arab countries anxiously waited for the results of the election, to know how they would prepare their agendas and strategies.

It is a fact that both Kerry and Bush are not admired greatly by Yemenis and are both not up to the expectations, especially when dealing with the Middle East conflict and the occupation of Iraq.

Nevertheless, I cannot but acknowledge the fascination of my Yemeni friends over the level of competition and overall democracy standard of the USA. They see that the advertising campaigns, the meetings with the public, the speeches, and the debates as a healthy indicator of a functioning democracy.

"It is something we can only dream of here in Yemen," was what my friend Ahmed told me the other day when comparing with presidential elections taking place in the Arab world, including Yemen.

On the other hand, Yemenis complain that the US has turned a blind eye to our agonies and frustration as Arabs under brutal dictatorships that have been kept in place with the support and encouragement of the West, topped by the USA.

"If it were not for the support the USA had been giving our regimes, I believe we would have been much better off today," Ahmed added.

It's obvious that George W. Bush is disliked by the majority of Yemenis due to the wars he launched in Afghanistan and Iraq. However, there is one action that most Yemenis liked about Bush, and that is his focus on helping democratize the Arab world after decades of negligence to this important element.

If there is one thing that Yemenis and I believe most Arabs would want to have continue in the US administration, is its persistence on continuing efforts to help reform the Arab world, to help it get out of stagnancy and have a better position in the world.

Let us hope that whoever comes out as the winner in this election will be a driving force for assisting reformists in the region and the world, to bring about a better future for each individual country, and the world as a whole.

The above articles were written prior to the election. What you are about to read are the articles that were published when President Bush was re-elected for a second term. Fasten your seatbelts. It's going to be a bumpy ride.

CHAPTER TWO

Carte Blanche to Murder

*T*his chapter is about the immediate reaction from the rest of the world to President Bush's re-election. The previous chapter concluded with the editorial from Yemen Times. Let's look at the reaction to the election result from another Yemen newspaper, the Yemen Observer.

There was also another incident that I considered worth sharing.

According to online encyclopedia Wikipedia *and other Yemen news sources, On February 11th 2006, chief editor of* Yemen Observer *Mohammed Al-Asadi was arrested on charges of offending Islam by republishing Danish cartoons of the Prophet Mohammed. The* Yemen Observer *claimed it only republished the cartoons—with a large X across them—in order to condemn them.*

Al-Asadi was released on bail on 22 February 2006. In a trial that began on 23 February 2006, prosecution lawyers called for Al-Asadi to be sentenced to death, for the paper to be closed and for all of its assets to be confiscated. Al-Asadi denied all charges and his defense team argued that the images were accompanied by articles that condemned the cartoons and reported reactions from across the Islamic world. The prosecution claimed that the charges rested on the pictures alone, and that the accompanying articles should not be taken into account. On December 6th 2006, Al-Asadi was convicted of insulting Islam, and fined YR 500,000. The paper was allowed to stay open, and Al-Asadi received no prison sentence. However, he was held at the courthouse in a holding cell until the fine was paid.

Why American Voters don't Care!

By Staff Editor – Yemen Observer
Nov 6, 2004 - Vol . VII Issue 44

Yemenis awoke Thursday afternoon to the not-so-unexpected news of American president George W. Bush's reelection to another four year term. While it is well within our rights as world citizens, subjected to the foreign policies of the lone superpower, to voice our disgust for the American people's decision and his policies, we should not let our vehement opposition veil what lessons and examples can be gleaned from the election results.

We must be careful to not assume that the American people's choice is an affirmation of current US policy in Iraq, Palestine, or the Middle East on whole. While to us the sole issue of importance is American foreign policy towards our region, for Americans it is only one issue within a long list that they decide upon. In fact, as polls show, the roughly 50% of American voters that supported Bush cared much more about domestic issues like homeland security, unemployment, taxes and the economy than international ones. Many Bush voters simply do not care about Iraq, or the Middle East, or Yemen for that matter, as evidenced by the Bush team's now seemingly successful attempt to make the Iraq War an issue of homeland security by trumping up the now infamous charges of

WMD and asserting what we now know to be weak to non-existent links between Saddam Hussein and Al-Qaeda.

Conversely, most of the other 51 million Americans that voted against Bush did have strong opposition to the current American policies in the Middle East. That means that just under half of voting Americans realize the negative consequences the current path has taken their country. Arabs are literally half way there to persuading all Americans that they matter.

Unfortunately for us, not enough of the Americans (just a few hundred thousand short in fact) seem to realize, or care, how their government's policies hurt Arabs. Instead, they are preoccupied with their own domestic concerns to be bothered by our woes across the world. But can we really blame them?

The Arab world is not exactly a model of democracy and government morality. While growing numbers of Americans are sympathetic, the average American sees our region as corrupt—which it is, Authoritarian—which it is, and oppressive—which it is. If we want Americans to care, if we want them to understand our suffering under their policy, we need to show them a region that cares about the same basic rights and freedoms that they do. How can we complain about a non—democratic, foreign installed government in Iraq, when that is the norm for the Arab region? Yemen, as the leader of democratic reform in Arabia, needs to push forward in its endeavor and urge our brotherly countries to follow suit. We need to give Americans something to care about.

We must be careful, however, that this need not be misinterpreted—that we don't cut off our nose to spite our face. We must realize that it is not possible to make Americans appreciate our humanity by lowering ourselves to the level of supporting inhumane acts of terrorism. We must differentiate our position of being opposed to the occupation in Iraq from supporting terrorist activities of some insurgent groups currently operating there; from being against the occupation of Israel to condoning bombing pizza restaurants and weddings. Anyone who would consider terrorist acts "justified" by American aggression in the region should watch just one of the horrific beheadings in Iraq, then ask themselves "do we really expect Americans to consider our suffering if we support these acts?"

If the adage is true that democracies don't invade democracies, than our best defense against an imperialistic, war-happy American policy is to democratize. Otherwise, Americans will always see their oppressive Arab foreign policy as only oppressing enemies of freedom who find it acceptable to saw off heads with kitchen knives.

GADO (Kenya) is the most Syndicated Political/Editorial cartoonist in the East and Central Africa.

The Bitter Pill of American Democracy

The following column appeared in numerous publications around the globe. I came across this article in several regional Indian and Bangladeshi newspapers, including in a daily newspaper published in Indian Kashmir. The author is an associate professor of history at UCLA.

Bitter pill of American democracy
Prof. Vinay Lal

The recently concluded American elections, which have given George W. Bush the victorious verdict that he so vigorously sought, are already being touted as the most marvelous demonstration of the success and robustness of American democracy.

The lines to vote were reported to be unusually long in many places around the country, the prolific predictions about fraud, voting irregularities, and the unreliability of electronic voting machines nearly all fell flat, a record number of new (mostly young) voters made their presence felt at the polls, and more Americans cast their vote than at any time since 1968. The usual platitudes, calling upon all Americans to "unite" after a bitterly divisive election campaign, were heard from Senator Kerry in his concession speech, and once again Bush, that archangel of "compassionate conservatism", has promised his opponent's supporters that he will attempt to win their trust. Only the future lies ahead of this, as Bush puts it, "amazing country".

Quite to the contrary, these elections furnish the most decisive illustration of the sheer mockery that electoral democracy has become in America. The iconoclastic American thinker, Paul Goodman, observed four decades ago in his "Compulsory Miseducation" that American democracy serves no other purpose than to help citizens distinguish between "indistinguishable candidates".

Both parties are utterly beholden to the culture of the corporation and what used to be called 'monied interests', and both have contributed to bloated military budgets; besides, however short the memory of those who fetishize Democrats as paragons of liberalism, decency, and civility. Democratic administrations have been scarcely reticent in exercising military power to subjugate enemies or ensure American dominance. Many Democrats held Ralph Nader, who understands better than most people the elaborate hoax by means of which one party has been masquerading as two for a very long time, responsible for sprinting votes away from Al Gore in 2000.

This served as one long-lasting excuse to which the Democrats could resort to explain why Gore was unable to prevail at the polls, and also explains why they went to extraordinary lengths to keep him from appearing on ballots in 2004; the other excuse originated in the circumstances under which a tenacious Bush, whose ambition for power is just as ruthless as his ignorance and arrogance are colossal, was able to get his brother Jeb Bush and the Supreme Court to hand over the White House to him. The dictators who run banana republics were doubtless imbibing a very different meaning from the axiom that America leads the way.

The present elections have blown these excuses, under which the Democrats have been sheltering and smoldering, to smithereens. Bush's victory margin, by the standards of democracy, is very large. Nader, the so-called "spoiler" and "traitor", won a mere few hundred thousand votes, and his presence doubtless even emboldened more Democrats to go to the polls. If Americans could not much distinguish between Bush and Kerry, and indeed how could they when Kerry, with his promise to "hunt down" the terrorists and wipe them from the face of this earth, sounded entirely like his opponent, the Democrats must ponder how they could have moved so far to the right and thus surrendered what little remains of their identity.

Considering the horrendous record that Bush has compiled in nearly every domain of national life—an illegal war of aggression against Iraq, the occupation of a sovereign nation, the strident embrace of militarism, the reckless disregard for the environment, the shameless pandering to the wealthy, the transformation of a 5-trillion dollar surplus into a 400-billion dollar deficit, the erosion of civil liberties, and much else—one cannot but conclude that the American people have given Bush carte blanche to do more of the same. Even the English language has not been spared by the Butcher of Crawford.

Bush's election means, in stark terms, that the majority of Americans condone the torture and indefinite confinement of suspects, the abrogation of international conventions, and an indefinite war—of terror, not just on terror—against nameless and numberless suspects. No extenuating circumstances can be pleaded on behalf of Americans, however much progressive intellectuals might like to think that Americans are fundamentally "good" and merely "misinformed" by the corporate media.

Those even more critical of Bush are inclined to view him as a liar. There is, however, scarcely any politician in the world who does not lie, though one can say of Bush that he almost always lies. But what if the American electorate understood his lies to be desirable, necessary, and premonitions of truth? Bush lied to the world about the presence of weapons of mass destruction in Iraq, he lied about the purported imminence of a threat against the United States from Iraq, and he falsely claimed a link between the al-Qaeda network and Iraq. Yet none of these revelations about the insidious modes in which consent is manufactured made an iota of difference, and Bush charged ahead with insistent reiterations of the same falsehoods.

The success of Bush points, in other words, to something much more ominous, namely the sheer inability of Americans to comprehend complexity and retain some degree of moral ambivalence. The fear that Bush is charged with exploiting, namely the fear of terrorism, is more broadly the fear of the unknown, the fear of ambiguity. Such exhortations to simplicity and unadorned moral fervor, and clear invocations of authoritarianism, couched as messages to people to entrust themselves into the hands of tried leaders who are hard on crime and terror, have in the past unfailingly furnished the recipe for transition to anti-democratic, even totalitarian, regimes.

Elections in India have consequences mainly for the Indian subcontinent, just as those in Australia largely impact Australia. But the American elections impact every person in the world, and there are clearly compelling reasons why every adult in the world should be allowed to vote in an American presidential election. However much every American might balk at this suggestion, it is indisputable, as the striking examples of Vietnam, Cambodia, Laos, Nicaragua, El Salvador, Afghanistan, and Iraq so vividly demonstrate, that the United States has never considered sovereignty an inviolable fact of international politics. It is no secret that the defeat of George Bush was, from the standpoint of the world, a consummation devoutly to be wished for. Many well-meaning Americans deride Bush as an "embarrassment". Used with reference to him, the word sounds like an encomium.

What's the Matter with America?

I'm sure many of you have read Thomas Frank's bestselling book, What's the Matter with Kansas? *Here is a fascinating article from Bangladesh that mimics the concept and title of Thomas Frank's book. The writer, Zafar Sobhan, is an assistant editor of the* Daily Star *of Bangladesh.*

What's the matter with America?
Zafar Sobhan
Daily Star of Bangladesh
Nov 5th 2004

There is a book out right now called What's the Matter with Kansas? by Thomas Frank in which the author explores the issue of why it is that so many middle and low-income Americans consistently vote Republican even though to do so is manifestly against their own economic interests.

Franks' explanation is interesting. He suggests that there is such little difference between Democrats and Republicans on economic issues that much of the electorate makes its decisions based largely on social and cultural issues.

The Republicans have proved adept at stoking up cultural anger in middle America against East coast elites, and keep winning elections by basing their appeal on a raft of social issues such as guns and abortion. These social issues resonate with the party faithful and get them to the polls in record numbers, as happened in 2004.

The point is to keep the fires of resentment burning against a liberal East coast elite trying to impose its values on the heartland, so that the heartland cultural conservatives are motivated to turn out in droves on election day to vote against Democrats — the party which is seen as the embodiment of such elitism.

Frank further suggests that the Democrats have no one but themselves to blame for this, and that the solution for them is to put forward more populist economic policies that would counteract the appeals to cultural and social issues made by the Republicans.

However, this is where his analysis breaks down, and there is no real support for his contention that if Democrats shifted to the left on economic issues that this would incline culturally conservative voters to give them another look.

In addition, let me suggest that, contrary to Frank's confident assertion, there do exist significant differences between the two parties on economic matters.

The one thing that Frank does not or perhaps cannot mention when he writes about the dominance of the Republican party in the heartland states is that the Republican strategy for victory is predicated on the essential baseness of the electorate in these states.

There is nothing intrinsically wrong with voting on cultural and social issues rather than economic ones—but the question Frank should be asking is what kind of social issues motivate these voters and what does this tell us about them.

And now that President Bush has won re-election by a comfortable margin, the question that I think needs to be asked is not what is wrong with Kansas, but what is wrong with the US as a whole.

There is no way to spin the election outcome positively for the Democrats. The election has been an endorsement of President Bush. Not a resounding mandate perhaps, but convincing enough.

Bush received nearly sixty million votes—the most in US history—and the Republicans picked up seats in the House and Senate. In 2000, Bush lost the popular vote by half a million, but this year his winning margin was over three and a half million, and he won 51 per cent of the popular vote.

Nor can anyone argue that the US electorate didn't know what it was getting. In 2000, Bush was something of an unknown quantity, but in 2004, everyone knows what kind of a man he is and where he stands on the issues.

So let's look at how and why he won and what a Bush victory says about the American people.

There were a number of key issues in the 2004 elections—the economy, the president's leadership in the war on terror including the war in Iraq, and social issues such as gay marriage.

In the end, the economy proved to be a wash. Even some states such as Ohio which lost hundreds of thousands of jobs on Bush's watch ended up going for him, and exit polls show that slightly more voters trusted Bush with the economy than Kerry.

In the end it all came down to Bush's leadership in the war on terror including the war in Iraq and the social issues.

Exit polls suggest that an overwhelming majority of voters believed that Bush would do a better job in the war on terror than Kerry.

In fact the exit polls make for alarming reading. This election was not a fluke. President Bush won because quite clearly more Americans agree with his policies and vision than with those of Senator Kerry.

The simple fact is that it didn't bother the electorate that Bush had run a mendacious and underhanded campaign against Kerry. In fact, more people thought that the Kerry campaign had been unfair than the other way around.

It didn't matter to the electorate that Bush had misled the country into war and has since then sensationally mishandled the continuing occupation. It didn't matter to the electorate that the stature of the country outside its borders stands at an all-time low. It didn't matter to the electorate that the invasion of Iraq has made the US far less safe from terror and that Bush has consistently underfunded and politicised homeland security as well.

In fact, a majority of Americans agreed with President Bush that the war on Iraq is an essential front in the war on terror and approved of the decision to go to war.

Bush won because on most of the important issues most of the American people agreed with him and not Kerry.

Nor should one discount the impact of cultural and social issues. This year the big issue was gay marriage. Initiatives to ban gay marriage passed in all eleven of the states in which they were on the ballot, and the issue brought conservative voters to the polls in record numbers. Millions of evangelicals who stayed home in 2000 came out to vote in 2004 based on their opposition to gay marriage and this helps to explain Bush's margin of victory.

In retrospect, the Massachusetts Supreme Court decision legalising gay marriage was one of the turning points in the election. It was this that brought the issue of gay marriage to the forefront of the public mind and mobilised conservative voters to turn out to vote in the numbers they did.

Even though he too opposes gay marriage—the fact that Senator Kerry is from Massachusetts couldn't have helped him with these voters, who overwhelmingly voted for President Bush.

The exit poll results on questions such as Bush's leadership and Iraq and "moral values" show that the time has come for the Democratic party to stop wringing its hands in despair and wondering what it can do to appeal better to voters in middle America.

If more Americans trust the economy to Bush than to Kerry despite the evidence of the past four years, if more Americans believe that the war in Iraq has made them safer, if more Americans believe that Bush is a steadfast and rock-ribbed leader in the war on terror, if more Americans believe that the most important thing is to deny civil rights to homosexuals, if more Americans believe that the president served more honourably than Kerry in Vietnam — then the Democrats can't win.

The problem is not with the Democratic party. The problem is with the American people.

After all, this is a people more than 40 percent of whom still think that there was a link between Saddam Hussein and 9/11 and almost 50 percent of whom think that things are going well for the US in Iraq.

There isn't much you can do about an electorate so deeply mired in delusion and denial.

I have always told my American friends that most people around the world do not dislike America—only the Republican party and its policies.

Most people around the world are quite capable of distinguishing between the people of a country and their leadership. But in a democracy at some point the people have to take responsibility for the man who is elected by them.

George Bush is clearly the American people's choice for president. Sixty million votes. The most in US history. More than Ronald Reagan ever received. 51 per cent of the popular vote. More than Bill Clinton ever received.

Perhaps the electorate could have been forgiven for 2000. No one knew for sure how bad Bush would be. Plus there is a good argument to be made that he didn't really win in the first place and certainly he lost the popular vote.

But not this time. This time—much as it pains me to admit— Bush seems to have won fair and square.

To my American friends—you are always asking why people don't like Americans. Perhaps this is why.

Steve Nease, Oakville, Ontario, Canada

A Message from Egypt

While Zaffar Shoban was trying to draw a balance, halfway around the globe another editorial from Egypt points out the role the U.S. should play in the Middle East. The following editorial was published by Cairo Press Review, *a government controlled portal that publishes a summary of Egyptian newspapers.*

Cairo Press Review
Nov 5th 2004

The American people failed to see how President Bush's war policy unaided by the skill of diplomacy made America more unsafe. American people's safety does not lie in the situation within the United States alone. They also have no idea of how long years of Israeli oppression with us help on Palestinian Muslims forced Muslims to counter terrorism. British Prime Minister Tony Blair could not have been more right when he emphasised while congratulating Bush on his reelection that crisis in the Middle East is the most pressing problem for the world and must be addressed.

President Bush during his first term appeared too eager to attack Iran for its nuclear programme for the need of energy while doing nothing about North Korea which is already in possession of nuclear weapons. Let us hope President Bush will pursue an unbiased policy toward nuclear proliferation. Bush administration must also give its contradiction over nuclear weapons possessed by Israel. His administration must also seriously examine the potential of private terrorism if the Muslim countries are rendered helpless against oppression of Muslims.

Land of Fears

Another Egyptian newspaper, Al-Akbar, *published an opinion written by a contributor, which took the analysis of the Middle Eastern reaction to another level. The article was published on the eve of Ohio results.*

Land of fears
By: Emad Omar
Al-Akhbar

Regardless of the result of the US presidential elections in Ohio and its effects on the Electoral College, the Republican candidate George W. Bush won a second term, a matter which stressed the fact that the US people were totally convinced of the message delivered by Bush during his campaign in which he spread out fears in the hearts of the Americans warning them against the threats of terrorism.

The fears of the US people reached the extent that they forgot about the merits of Kerry's platforms which focused mainly on improving the living standards of the majority of the US people.

Therefore, the Americans preferred security to bread, yet they paid no heed to the fact that by invading Iraq, Bush did weaken his war on terror besides smearing the image of the US as to friends and foes as well.

By accepting Bush's message, the majority of the US people proved that the US has turned from the land of dreams to the land of fears.

Four More Years of War?

The following opinion, written by Patrick Seale, a Paris-based political analyst and commentator was published by the Daily Star, *a pan-Middle East English language newspaper edited in Beirut, Lebanon and published alongside the* International Herald Tribune.

In 2004, the Daily Star *merged its Lebanon and Regional editions choosing to focus on Lebanese expatriates in the Gulf Cooperation Council (GCC) region. Now, the unified edition appears in all countries except for Kuwait which has its own local edition published in partnership with* Al-Watan, *a Kuwaiti Arabic language daily.*

In 2006, the newspaper announced that its paper will soon be available in print in the United States.

Patrick Seale was born in Belfast, Northern Ireland and currently lives in Paris. He is the author of The Struggle for Syria; *and* Asad of Syria: The Struggle for the Middle East *and* Abu Nidal: A Gun for Hire.

And now ... 4 more years of war?
By Patrick Seale
Special to The Daily Star - Lebanon
Thursday, November 04, 2004

By putting George W. Bush back in the White House for four more years, the American electorate has voted for war. This is the single most important outcome of the American presidential election.

The American public knows it is already at war - at war in Iraq; at war against "global terror;" at war against Osama bin Laden and against the new "bogeyman," Abu Mussab al-Zarqawi; at war against all those who would challenge American supremacy; at war against Islam itself!

A majority of Americans sees Bush as the strong commander in chief who can lead his country to victory. They want him to kill America's enemies, as he has promised to do.

This is an alarming prospect for much of the rest of the world which tends to see the war in Iraq as a catastrophic mistake and Bush's global "war on terror" as a dangerously misleading slogan. But the facts need to be faced: still traumatized by Sept. 11, America is in the grip of fear and rage.

Frightened at the possibility of further terrorist attacks, obsessed with security yet drunk with its immense power, America is enraged beyond reason that its puny enemies have dared strike at its once inviolable homeland. It does not want a dialogue with these enemies, still less a negotiation. It does not recognise that they have any legitimate grievance. It wants them destroyed. And it believes Bush is the man to do it.

There is another major reason for Bush's victory, and it lies in the belief of many Americans that God is on his side — a conviction Bush, a born-again Christian, has not hesitated to proclaim. His sense of divine mission is typical of the religious mindset which now characterises much of America — its vast rural communities rather than its secular cities.

Christian fundamentalism — belief in the Bible as the literal word of God — is one manifestation of the slide toward conservative values which has taken place in America over recent decades and which has resulted in opposition to abortion, gay marriage and stem-cell research. In his campaign, Bush has exploited these socially divisive issues as he has America's fear of terrorist attack.

The world must now come to terms not just with the Bush they have known, ridiculed and hated over the past four years, the Bush they hoped would be defeated, but with a far stronger Bush, whose Republican party controls all three branches of government — the presidency, the Congress (where he has a comfortable majority in both the House of Representatives and the Senate) and, more ominously for civil rights, the Supreme Court.

Rather than the traditional balance of power between the White House and the Congress, a balance which would usually require negotiation and accommodation to get legislation passed, America has one-party control of its national government.

How will a victorious Bush behave? Some optimists believe that, at home, he will moderate his right-wing views and reach out to the Democrats in a bid to unify a deeply divided nation. The same optimists believe that, abroad, he will seek to heal the transatlantic rift and ease America's strained relations with France and Germany, the main critics of his Iraq war.

Some even go so far as to recall that Bush himself at one time called for a Palestinian state. Freed from the need to court the Jewish vote, might he not now relaunch the moribund Middle East peace process and pressure Israel to start serious negotiations with the Palestinians?

All this is highly unlikely. Even if Bush were inclined to correct his aim - of which there is no sign — he would probably be prevented from doing so by Vice President Dick Cheney, the strongman of his administration. Whatever changes Bush may make in his Cabinet, the hard-line Cheney is an immovable fixture.

A more likely outcome is that Bush's personal triumph — including his large share of the popular vote — will convince him that he has been "chosen" to implement an unashamedly ideological agenda. This will mean turning back the clock on environmental protection, health insurance and other socially progressive issues at home, while continuing to pursue a tough unilateralist foreign policy, reliant principally on military force.

This is good news for some, bad news for others.

Russian President Vladimir Putin and Israeli Prime Minister Ariel Sharon have made no secret of their support for Bush. They will be jubilant at his re-election. Unlike the Democrats, Bush has not criticised Putin for his criminal repression of Chechnya and for his increasingly authoritarian style of government. Nor has Bush criticised Sharon for his equally criminal repression of the Palestinians. Israel killed 165 Palestinians last month, many of them civilians.

The new orthodoxy — repeated on Nov. 3 by Israeli Foreign Minister Silvan Shalom in an article in the French daily, *Le Monde* — is that the U.S., Russia and Israel are fighting the same Islamic terrorists and must stand together. Shalom included Indonesia and Turkey in the club and called on Europe to join it, seeing that it was, in his words, "equally threatened by the tyranny of terrorism and radical fundamentalism."

Bush's victory is viewed with considerable apprehension in Old Europe, where the call is now for a stronger, more tightly integrated Europe to act as a counterweight to America. The fear is that Bush will persist in his same bankrupt policies, pursuing them even more intensely than before.

In Iraq, this will mean renewed efforts to crush the insurgency by force, including the shelling and aerial bombardment of Fallujah and other cities. If 100,000 Iraqis have already lost their lives since the American invasion in March 2003, how many more will have to die before America comes to its senses? Several European and Arab leaders — including King Abdullah of Jordan, an American ally - believe that the only solution lies in reconstituting the old Iraqi Army under Iraqi command. It is the only institution able to restore security and hold the country together. An essential precondition would be for the U.S. to announce a firm date for the withdrawal of its forces — and keep to it.

The Palestinians have every reason to be deeply concerned at Bush's victory. Even if he were to sack some prominent pro-Sharon ideologues from his team — which is by no means certain as he might even promote them — the right—wing U.S.-Israeli alliance will be as firm as ever.

The U.S. has endorsed Sharon's position that he will not negotiate with the Palestinians until they abandon all resistance, in other words until they surrender. Militant groups like Hamas are unlikely to comply. The bitter struggle is set to continue, with great pain and damage to all sides.

Even more disturbing to international peace is the armed confrontation between the United States and the world-wide Islamic insurgency, of which Osama bin Laden is the symbol, if not the operational commander. He is the archetype of the non-state actors who have emerged because of the inability and unwillingness of Arab regimes to deter or contain both U.S. and Israeli aggression.

There have been many American interpretations of bin Laden's latest video lecture, most of them dismissive. "We are fighting you," bin Laden said, "because you attacked us and continue to attack us. ... You attacked us in Palestine. ...You attacked us in Somalia; you supported the Russian atrocities against us in Chechnya, the Indian oppression against us in Kashmir, and the Jewish aggression against us in Lebanon."

These grievances strike a chord with most Arabs and Muslims.

One phrase escaped the attention of the commentators. Addressing America, bin Laden declared: "We call on you to deal with us and interact with us on the basis of mutual interests and benefits." What is this if not an invitation to negotiate?

A wise American president would heed such calls, revise his policies and seek to make his peace with militant Islam. Not so, George W Bush!

Four More Years in the Bush

The following column was published in the Jamaican Observer *soon after the election. Barbara Gloudon is a senior Jamaican journalist, and has long been involved in the arts, especially Jamaica's* Little Theatre Movement *and the annual* Jamaica Pantomime. *She has held editorial positions with the Gleaner publications, was a Deputy Director of Tourism, and is currently senior host on the Jamaican public affairs talk show* Hotline. *She is the holder of various honors including the Order of Jamaica and the D.Litt (Honoris Causa) from the University of the West Indies.*

Four more years in the Bush
Barbara Gloudon
Jamaica Observer
Friday, November 05, 2004

NOVEMBER 2, 2004 is set to enter the history books as another day when Atlas shrugged. George the Second was returned to the White House throne and America showed the rest of the world that the American people, not world opinion, would decide what was good for America.

If the miles of commentary written in almost every language, the endless hours of television, the rubber hitting the road on the information highway, was anything to go by, the reign of George W Bush should have ended on Tuesday. But it didn't. The son of a Bush is all set to rule the world for another four years — and those who don't like it, can do what they can to heal their "achey-breakey heart" or lump it.

Last weekend this time, Mr Bush's fate was the catalyst for a media feeding frenzy around the world. You couldn't turn on the TV and not see some programme or other focusing on the Bush Factor. Some people wanted him out of the Oval Office so much that they threw all caution to the wind and let rip with contemptuous criticism. "For the preservation of world peace, the wretched man must go. So, too, should his best friend Tony Blair and other suck-ups who are backing him in this dreadful war."

One of the more interesting online litmus tests of Bush-rating was a poll by a source titled BetaVote.com which invited people from some 240 nations around the globe to react to the question. "What if the whole world could vote in the US Presidential election?" Jamaica was among them and registered 69 per cent approval for John Kerry. A pattern of overwhelming response to Kerry was established, with the exception of the African nation state of Niger (pronounce it Ni-jah or Nee-jare as you will). It was the ONLY nation which voted for Bush.

In a few other places (Barbados for example), opinion was "statistically even" between the candidates. With this kind of response repeated over the hours leading up to poll day, Kerry supporters seemed certain that their man was the one. But, you know what they say — it ain't over till the fat lady sings and sing she did, a whole opera spanning the gamut of emotions and a nail-biting prologue.

Come we now to four more years of Bush rule, four more years of the Democrats wondering what they did wrong this time, four more years for the world to get it through its head that America Rules. "Apocalypse now!" the fearful have already started to cry. Will Cuba be attacked? What about Iran? Will we be singing "So much trouble in the world" and "War, everywhere is war?" It would be interesting to know what Mr Bush thinks of world opinion, why some people should be scared at the prospects of so much power concentrated in the hands of one man, one nation. True, there are supposed to be checks and balances, like the United Nations, right? Yeah. Right. On the other hand, maybe the rest of the world is behaving like Chicken Little and the sky ain't even falling. Give an old cliché its due. Time will tell.

ONE GROUP of people within the American society for which November 2 held much significance was the Caribbean American population. By all accounts, our people are beginning to "come of age", emerging from the shadows of "single entry", regularising their status, entering the mainstream and in true Caribbean style, making their presence felt.

A significant factor is the presence of young born-in-the-USA sons and daughters of the Caribbean who are laying claim to the American Dream in all its manifestations, political power included. (One is tempted to say that they are playing a more dynamic role in their milieu than their counterparts back here, but that is for another day). Reports coming out of some of the areas where our people have established a presence, show that they did not take November 2 lightly. They heeded to the call to be registered to vote and vote they did, Democrats for the most part, according to reports.

If conversations which I had with two sets of people in New York and Ft Lauderdale on Wednesday are any indicator, Caribbean people were Kerry people. It was not so much that they were moved by any strong personal commitment to him as how determined they were to remove Mr. Bush. Immigration is a big issue for them and the Bush regime did not weigh in heavily on that score. The result of the polls came as a bitter disappointment for them.

Some even expressed the view that their vote had been wasted and some said that they regretted that they had invested in campaigning and getting out the vote in their communities. Some predicted dark days ahead, especially as it concerns unemployment, neglect in the education of the poor, dubious health care and assorted other concerns, in which, they claim, Mr Bush and the Republicans seem to have no interest. Even avid Kerry supporters admitted, however, that their candidate was not all that strong on such issues, either. Both candidates seemed to choke on the word "poor".

Middle class was as far as they got.

ON THE OTHER HAND, not everyone was buried in pessimism. In the conversations on Wednesday, we spoke to two avid Bush supporters, both Jamaicans residing in New York. One voted Bush because he is convinced that he is going to make it big, thanks to the president's policy of tax relief for business. He discounted any argument which said Bush was only for the rich. In any case, ambitious Jamaican that he is, he has plans for moving up into a higher tax bracket as soon as possible.

The other pro-Busher said he went with him because of "moral values". Like Bush, he says, he is "anti-abortion, anti-homosexuality, anti-stem cell research".

When I asked how much he knew about stem-cell research, his answer revealed more than a little confusion about the precise details but as the saying goes, "Don't confuse me with the facts." The Brother said he was ecstatic at Mr Bush's victory and is "looking forward to four more good years under strong moral leadership".

Meanwhile, two women, also Jamaicans, who campaigned against Bush through their trade unions, said they see no cause for rejoicing. "I feel sick to my stomach," one said. They claim that the president is anti-labour, anti-worker. They see nothing but trouble ahead.

One hardly assumes that Mr Bush is losing any sleep over such observations. In his victory speech, he says he is embracing all Kerry supporters to place their trust in him. They have no choice. Nor do we, or much of the world for that matter.

Shock and Awe

The following piece is the follow-up to the original letter that was published in Pravda Online, *Russia. This is what Timothy Bancroft-Hinchey wrote after President Bush was re-elected.*

Shock and awe.
Timothy Bancroft-Hinchey
Pravda Online, Russia

The American people have decided to vote for four more years of the Bush regime. Only 1,460 days to go.

Incredible as it may seem, the people of the United States of America — or rather, just over half, have decided to go for broke: four more years of a Bush regime which has chalked up a 200 billion dollar bill to pay for its disaster in Iraq, four more years of a Bush regime which has been responsible for mass murder on a scale unseen since the Vietnam War, for breaking the UN Charter and the Geneva Convention and for divorcing the international community.

Yet the citizens of the United States of America, through a free and democratic process, have given their collective nod to more of the same, if indeed the process was fair.

In so doing, the citizens of the USA have taken upon themselves a collective responsibility for the consequences of what they have done. Four years ago, it could have been argued that nobody knew that the Bush regime would stand for lies, blackmail, forgery, murder, skullduggery, insulting the international community, launching a murderous act of butchery, slaughtering innocent civilians in their tens of thousands, dropping cluster bombs in civilian areas. Murdering women. Murdering kids.

Four years on, after the whole and horrific truth as to what the Bush regime was responsible for, nobody can claim that they were misled or that they did not know what they were voting for. Therefore, collectively, the people of the United States of America, or just over half of them, in voting for Bush have condoned his act of mass murder in Iraq, have condoned the shocking acts of torture in Abu Ghraib and elsewhere, have condoned the existence of the concentration camp at Guantanamo Bay, have condoned the deployment of military hardware against civilians, have condoned the acts of butchery in which US military personnel blasted the limbs of three-year-old boys and girls, have condoned the war crimes, have condoned the targeting of civilian structures with military hardware and have given the nod to the super-rich clique of corporate elitists which gravitate around the White House becoming richer and fatter by the minute as they dictate Washington's policy.

Four years on, the people of America have just bought, and put on, a collective cloak of responsibility which they will have to wear for four long years, and for which they will be held fully accountable by the rest of mankind.

Four years on, the citizens of America have voted for isolation, have voted against the collective wishes of the rest of humanity, which looks on in horror and disbelief at the results of an election in which George Bush would have received less than a third of the votes in 99% of the other members of the international community.

Four years on, the people who voted the Bush regime back into power have no excuses. They voted for lies, for mass murder, they voted for a person and a regime which turned its back on the rest of the world.

There are 300 million US citizens. There are six billion people in the international community. If the people of America have voted for a divorce, so be it. The rest of the world can get along fine. The tragedy is that just under half of the population, the good, clear-thinking Americans who saw through the Bush farce for what it is, will have to pay the consequences of the political blindness demonstrated by the other half. The result of November 2nd is a country divided between those who have any idea as to what they are doing and those who are apparently so easily fooled, an America divided between those who wanted to marry the international community and those who wished to divorce it.

The international community will never again allow the Bush regime to commit any further acts of butchery, therefore the influence of this election on world affairs is relative. The question is, whether the rest of the world will have anything to do with Washington now that the people have stubbornly given Bush a mandate.

The people of America have voted for more of the same. They made the bed they will lie in for the next 1,460 days.

The following editorial is from Daily Nation, Kenya. Daily Nation *was set up in 1959 by His Highness Prince Karim Aga Khan IV, the spiritual leader of the Ismaili community worldwide, and is the most influential newspaper in Kenya with a daily circulation of about 205,000 copies.*

Quagmire

Daily Nation
Kenya – Editorial

Kenyans yesterday joined the rest of the world in keeping a close watch on the US presidential election.

For many, in fact, the US polls have become like those major global events attracting massive worldwide audiences every four years, such as the Olympic Games and the soccer World Cup.

The US presidential election, of course, is much more serious than sport — even though it provides its fair share of that, complete with cliffhanger finales and on-field disputes.

In this unipolar world, the US president is by far the most powerful person in the world. He has the power to make the world a better place or, with the arsenal at his command, unleash a conflagration that can make Hiroshima look like a Sunday school picnic.

As Americans gave President George W. Bush the majority vote, the final result last night still hinged on the battle for Ohio's electoral vote.

But President Bush seems set for a second disputed term, and Americans might have noted that, elsewhere in the world, the clear preference was his Democratic Party challenger, John Kerry.

The rest of the world sees Mr Bush as a warmonger held in thrall by the fundamentalist Christian right and the military-industrial complex that holds sway in the US.

The world rightly grieved with America following the terrible terrorist attacks of 9/11. There was widespread international support for the subsequent US-led war on terror which started with the invasion of Afghanistan and the ouster of the Taliban regime which sheltered Osama bin Laden's al Qaeda terrorist network.

But as we came to painfully learn, Mr Bush's war on terror did not make the world safer. And then he went off-track when he launched another war against Iraq on the most dubious of grounds.

It has since been proved that the invasion was based on lies. There were no weapons of mass destruction in Iraq. Nor was there any evidence that President Saddam Hussein ever collaborated with Al Qaeda. This war has made Bush, and America, deeply unpopular across the world. Osama remains at large. The threat of international terrorism remains as real as ever. Though Al Qaeda may have been scattered in Afghanistan, Osama remains at large, attracting ever more fanatic adherents to his peculiar cause: War against the US and all its allies.

And while he may have been forced to lie low in hideouts, other terrorist leaders spread across the world have been able mobilise those who are even more inspired to resist America's military adventures.

An occupied Iraq has become more unstable and dangerous than at any time during Saddam's rule. And anti-Americanism has spread throughout the Arab and Muslim world, threatening many moderate regimes and US client-states.

In other words, the world is much more at risk of global terrorism than it ever was at the advent of the war on terror. It appears President Bush has made the world much more unsafe to live in.

Americans, of course, do not see it that way. This election was largely a referendum on the Bush administration's pursuit of the war on terror. By giving President Bush four more years, the American voters have given him a direct mandate to continue on the path he has pursued.

Denying him re-election would have been a clear message that Americans want to get out of the Iraqi quagmire.

Americans have the right to determine who will lead them in the style they interpret to reflect their national interests. Nobody can take that right away from them and nobody can determine for them what those interests are.

On Tuesday, they decided that keeping up the war on terror, and specifically holding on to the occupation of Iraq, was preferable to admitting defeat.

We can only respect their choice, even if we may be infuriated by a peculiarly American insularity that is at odds with what the rest of the world thinks.

Being president of the US comes with a great deal of responsibility. Whoever occupies that powerful office must realise that he is responsible to the global community and not just to narrow national interests.

Art, Truth, and Politics

The following article may surprise a lot of readers. The author, Harold Pinter, is the recipient of the 2005 Nobel Prize for literature, and this is his acceptance speech, delivered at the Nobel Foundation in Sweden. This particular speech has become so popular around the world that almost every country translated and reprinted it. Yet none of our American mass media outlets gave any prominence to this very important material, which many consider the most widely read Nobel acceptance speech ever. I read this in a community publication that I found in an Asian grocery store in Edison, New Jersey.

When I contacted the Nobel Foundation to get the reprint permission for this article, the team in Sweden was so helpful that I even forgot that I was communicating with one of the most prestigious institutions in the world. I realized how small (or 'flat' in Friedman's terms) the world has become.

Harold Pinter – Nobel Lecture
Art, Truth & Politics

In 1958 I wrote the following:

'There are no hard distinctions between what is real and what is unreal, nor between what is true and what is false. A thing is not necessarily either true or false; it can be both true and false.'

I believe that these assertions still make sense and do still apply to the exploration of reality through art. So as a writer I stand by them but as a citizen I cannot. As a citizen I must ask: What is true? What is false?

Truth in drama is forever elusive. You never quite find it but the search for it is compulsive. The search is clearly what drives the endeavour. The search is your task. More often than not you stumble upon the truth in the dark, colliding with it or just glimpsing an image or a shape which seems to correspond to the truth, often without realising that you have done so. But the real truth is that there never is any such thing as one truth to be found in dramatic art. There are many. These truths challenge each other, recoil from each other, reflect each other, ignore each other, tease each other, are blind to each other. Sometimes you feel you have the truth of a moment in your hand, then it slips through your fingers and is lost.

I have often been asked how my plays come about. I cannot say. Nor can I ever sum up my plays, except to say that this is what happened. That is what they said. That is what they did.

Political language, as used by politicians, does not venture into any of this territory since the majority of politicians, on the evidence available to us, are interested not in truth but in power and in the maintenance of that power. To maintain that power it is essential that people remain in ignorance, that they live in ignorance of the truth, even the truth of their own lives. What surrounds us therefore is a vast tapestry of lies, upon which we feed.

As every single person here knows, the justification for the invasion of Iraq was that Saddam Hussein possessed a highly dangerous body of weapons of mass destruction, some of which could be fired in 45 minutes, bringing about appalling devastation. We were assured that was true. It was not true. We were told that Iraq had a relationship with Al Quaeda and shared responsibility for the atrocity in New York of September 11th 2001. We were assured that this was true. It was not true. We were told that Iraq threatened the security of the world. We were assured it was true. It was not true.

The truth is something entirely different. The truth is to do with how the United States understands its role in the world and how it chooses to embody it.

But before I come back to the present I would like to look at the recent past, by which I mean United States foreign policy since the end of the Second World War. I believe it is obligatory upon us to subject this period to at least some kind of even limited scrutiny, which is all that time will allow here.

Everyone knows what happened in the Soviet Union and throughout Eastern Europe during the post-war period: the systematic brutality, the widespread atrocities, the ruthless suppression of independent thought. All this has been fully documented and verified.

But my contention here is that the US crimes in the same period have only been superficially recorded, let alone documented, let alone acknowledged, let alone recognised as crimes at all. I believe this must be addressed and that the truth has considerable bearing on where the world stands now. Although constrained, to a certain extent, by the existence of the Soviet Union, the United States' actions throughout the world made it clear that it had concluded it had carte blanche to do what it liked.

Direct invasion of a sovereign state has never in fact been America's favoured method. In the main, it has preferred what it has described as 'low intensity conflict'. Low intensity conflict means that thousands of people die but slower than if you dropped a bomb on them in one fell swoop. It means that you infect the heart of the country, that you establish a malignant growth and watch the gangrene bloom. When the populace has been subdued – or beaten to death – the same thing – and your own friends, the military and the great corporations, sit comfortably in power, you go before the camera and say that democracy has prevailed. This was a commonplace in US foreign policy in the years to which I refer.

The tragedy of Nicaragua was a highly significant case. I choose to offer it here as a potent example of America's view of its role in the world, both then and now.

I was present at a meeting at the US embassy in London in the late 1980s.

The United States Congress was about to decide whether to give more money to the Contras in their campaign against the state of Nicaragua. I was a member of a delegation speaking on behalf of Nicaragua but the most important member of this delegation was a Father John Metcalf. The leader of the US body was Raymond Seitz (then number two to the ambassador, later ambassador himself). Father Metcalf said: 'Sir, I am in charge of a parish in the north of Nicaragua. My parishioners built a school, a health centre, a cultural centre. We have lived in peace. A few months ago a Contra force attacked the parish. They destroyed everything: the school, the health centre, the cultural centre. They raped nurses and teachers, slaughtered doctors, in the most brutal manner. They behaved like savages. Please demand that the US government withdraw its support from this shocking terrorist activity.'

Raymond Seitz had a very good reputation as a rational, responsible and highly sophisticated man. He was greatly respected in diplomatic circles. He listened, paused and then spoke with some gravity. 'Father,' he said, 'let me tell you something. In war, innocent people always suffer.' There was a frozen silence. We stared at him. He did not flinch.

Innocent people, indeed, always suffer.

Finally somebody said: 'But in this case "innocent people" were the victims of a gruesome atrocity subsidised by your government, one among many. If Congress allows the Contras more money further atrocities of this kind will take place. Is this not the case? Is your government not therefore guilty of supporting acts of murder and destruction upon the citizens of a sovereign state?'

Seitz was imperturbable. 'I don't agree that the facts as presented support your assertions,' he said.

As we were leaving the Embassy a US aide told me that he enjoyed my plays. I did not reply.

I should remind you that at the time President Reagan made the following statement: 'The Contras are the moral equivalent of our Founding Fathers.'

The United States supported the brutal Somoza dictatorship in Nicaragua for over 40 years. The Nicaraguan people, led by the Sandinistas, overthrew this regime in 1979, a breathtaking popular revolution.

The Sandinistas weren't perfect. They possessed their fair share of arrogance and their political philosophy contained a number of contradictory elements. But they were intelligent, rational and civilised. They set out to establish a stable, decent, pluralistic society. The death penalty was abolished. Hundreds of thousands of poverty-stricken peasants were brought back from the dead. Over 100,000 families were given title to land. Two thousand schools were built. A quite remarkable literacy campaign reduced illiteracy in the country to less than one seventh. Free education was established and a free health service. Infant mortality was reduced by a third. Polio was eradicated.

The United States denounced these achievements as Marx-ist/Leninist subversion. In the view of the US government, a dangerous example was being set. If Nicaragua was allowed to establish basic norms of social and economic justice, if it was allowed to raise the standards of health care and education and achieve social unity and national self respect, neighbouring countries would ask the same questions and do the same things. There was of course at the time fierce resistance to the status quo in El Salvador.

I spoke earlier about 'a tapestry of lies' which surrounds us. President Reagan commonly described Nicaragua as a 'totalitarian dungeon'. This was taken generally by the media, and certainly by the British government, as accurate and fair comment. But there was in fact no record of death squads under the Sandinista government. There was no record of torture. There was no record of systematic or official military brutality. No priests were ever murdered in

79

Nicaragua. There were in fact three priests in the government, two Jesuits and a Maryknoll missionary. The totalitarian dungeons were actually next door, in El Salvador and Guatemala. The United States had brought down the democratically elected government of Guatemala in 1954 and it is estimated that over 200,000 people had been victims of successive military dictatorships.

Six of the most distinguished Jesuits in the world were viciously murdered at the Central American University in San Salvador in 1989 by a battalion of the Alcatl regiment trained at Fort Benning, Georgia, USA. That extremely brave man Archbishop Romero was assassinated while saying mass. It is estimated that 75,000 people died. Why were they killed? They were killed because they believed a better life was possible and should be achieved. That belief immediately qualified them as communists. They died because they dared to question the status quo, the endless plateau of poverty, disease, degradation and oppression, which had been their birthright.

The United States finally brought down the Sandinista government. It took some years and considerable resistance but relentless economic persecution and 30,000 dead finally undermined the spirit of the Nicaraguan people. They were exhausted and poverty stricken once again. The casinos moved back into the country. Free health and free education were over. Big business returned with a vengeance. 'Democracy' had prevailed.

But this 'policy' was by no means restricted to Central America. It was conducted throughout the world. It was never-ending. And it is as if it never happened.

The United States supported and in many cases engendered every right wing military dictatorship in the world after the end of the Second World War. I refer to Indonesia, Greece, Uruguay, Brazil, Paraguay, Haiti, Turkey, the Philippines, Guatemala, El Salvador, and, of course, Chile. The horror the United States inflicted upon Chile in 1973 can never be purged and can never be forgiven.

Hundreds of thousands of deaths took place throughout these countries. Did they take place? And are they in all cases attributable to US foreign policy? The answer is yes they did take place and they are attributable to American foreign policy. But you wouldn't know it.

It never happened. Nothing ever happened. Even while it was happening it wasn't happening. It didn't matter. It was of no interest. The crimes of the United States have been systematic, constant, vicious, remorseless, but very few people have actually talked about them. You have to hand it to America. It has exercised a quite clinical manipulation of power worldwide while masquerading as a force for universal good. It's a brilliant, even witty, highly successful act of hypnosis.

I put to you that the United States is without doubt the greatest show on the road. Brutal, indifferent, scornful and ruthless it may be but it is also very clever. As a salesman it is out on its own and its most saleable commodity is self love. It's a winner. Listen to all American presidents on television say the words, 'the American people', as in the sentence, 'I say to the American people it is time to pray and to defend the rights of the American people and I ask the American people to trust their president in the action he is about to take on behalf of the American people.'

It's a scintillating stratagem. Language is actually employed to keep thought at bay. The words 'the American people' provide a truly voluptuous cushion of reassurance. You don't need to think. Just lie back on the cushion. The cushion may be suffocating your intelligence and your critical faculties but it's very comfortable. This does not apply of course to the 40 million people living below the poverty line and the 2 million men and women imprisoned in the vast gulag of prisons, which extends across the US.

The United States no longer bothers about low intensity conflict. It no longer sees any point in being reticent or even devious. It puts its cards on the table without fear or favour. It quite simply doesn't give a damn about the United Nations, international law or critical dissent, which it regards as impotent and irrelevant. It also has its own bleating little lamb tagging behind it on a lead, the pathetic and supine Great Britain.

What has happened to our moral sensibility? Did we ever have any? What do these words mean? Do they refer to a term very rarely employed these days – conscience? A conscience to do not only with our own acts but to do with our shared responsibility in the acts of others? Is all this dead? Look at Guantanamo Bay. Hundreds of people detained without charge for over three years, with no legal representation or due process, technically detained forever. This totally illegitimate structure is maintained in defiance of the Geneva Convention. It is not only tolerated but hardly thought about by what's called the 'international community'. This criminal outrage is being committed by a country, which declares itself to be 'the leader of the free world'. Do we think about the inhabitants of Guantanamo Bay? What does the media say about them? They pop up occasionally – a small item on page six. They have been consigned to a no man's land from which indeed they may never return. At present many are on hunger strike, being force-fed, including British residents. No niceties in these force-feeding procedures. No sedative or anaesthetic. Just a tube stuck up your nose and into your throat. You vomit blood. This is torture. What has the British Foreign Secretary said about this? Nothing. What has the British Prime Minister said about this? Nothing. Why not? Because the United States has said: to criticise our conduct in Guantanamo Bay constitutes an unfriendly act. You're either with us or against us. So Blair shuts up.

The invasion of Iraq was a bandit act, an act of blatant state terrorism, demonstrating absolute contempt for the concept of international law. The invasion was an arbitrary military action inspired by a series of lies upon lies and gross manipulation of the media and therefore of the public; an act intended to consolidate

American military and economic control of the Middle East masquerading – as a last resort – all other justifications having failed to justify themselves – as liberation. A formidable assertion of military force responsible for the death and mutilation of thousands and thousands of innocent people.

We have brought torture, cluster bombs, depleted uranium, innumerable acts of random murder, misery, degradation and death to the Iraqi people and call it 'bringing freedom and democracy to the Middle East'.

How many people do you have to kill before you qualify to be described as a mass murderer and a war criminal? One hundred thousand? More than enough, I would have thought. Therefore it is just that Bush and Blair be arraigned before the International Criminal Court of Justice. But Bush has been clever. He has not ratified the International Criminal Court of Justice. Therefore if any American soldier or for that matter politician finds himself in the dock Bush has warned that he will send in the marines. But Tony Blair has ratified the Court and is therefore available for prosecution. We can let the Court have his address if they're interested. It is Number 10, Downing Street, London.

Death in this context is irrelevant. Both Bush and Blair place death well away on the back burner. At least 100,000 Iraqis were killed by American bombs and missiles before the Iraq insurgency began. These people are of no moment. Their deaths don't exist. They are blank. They are not even recorded as being dead. 'We don't do body counts,' said the American general Tommy Franks.

Early in the invasion there was a photograph published on the front page of British newspapers of Tony Blair kissing the cheek of a little Iraqi boy. 'A grateful child,' said the caption. A few days later there was a story and photograph, on an inside page, of another four-year-old boy with no arms. His family had been blown up by a missile. He was the only survivor. 'When do I get my arms back?' he asked. The story was dropped. Well, Tony Blair wasn't holding him

in his arms, nor the body of any other mutilated child, nor the body
of any bloody corpse. Blood is dirty. It dirties your shirt and tie when
you're making a sincere speech on television.

The 2,000 American dead are an embarrassment. They are
transported to their graves in the dark. Funerals are unobtrusive, out
of harm's way. The mutilated rot in their beds, some for the rest of
their lives. So the dead and the mutilated both rot, in different kinds
of graves.

Here is an extract from a poem by Pablo Neruda,

'I'm Explaining a Few Things':

And one morning all that was burning,
one morning the bonfires leapt out of the earth
devouring human beings and from then on fire,
gunpowder from then on, and from then on blood.

Bandits with planes and Moors,
bandits with finger-rings and duchesses,
bandits with black friars spattering blessings
came through the sky to kill children
and the blood of children ran through the streets
without fuss, like children's blood.

Jackals that the jackals would despise
stones that the dry thistle would bite on and spit out,
vipers that the vipers would abominate.

Face to face with you I have seen the blood
of Spain tower like a tide
to drown you in one wave of pride and knives.

Treacherous generals:
see my dead house, look at broken Spain:
from every house burning metal flows
instead of flowers from every socket of Spain

Spain emerges
and from every dead child a rifle with eyes
and from every crime bullets are born
which will one day find
the bull's eye of your hearts.

And you will ask: why doesn't his poetry
speak of dreams and leaves
and the great volcanoes of his native land.

Come and see the blood in the streets.
Come and see the blood in the streets.
Come and see the blood in the streets!

Let me make it quite clear that in quoting from Neruda's poem I am in no way comparing Republican Spain to Saddam Hussein's Iraq. I quote Neruda because nowhere in contemporary poetry have I read such a powerful visceral description of the bombing of civilians.

I have said earlier that the United States is now totally frank about putting its cards on the table. That is the case. Its official declared policy is now defined as 'full spectrum dominance'. That is not my term, it is theirs. 'Full spectrum dominance' means control of land, sea, air and space and all attendant resources.

The United States now occupies 702 military installations throughout the world in 132 countries, with the honourable exception of Sweden, of course. We don't quite know how they got there but they are there all right.

The United States possesses 8,000 active and operational nuclear warheads. Two thousand are on hair trigger alert, ready to be launched with 15 minutes warning. It is developing new systems of nuclear force, known as bunker busters. The British, ever cooperative, are intending to replace their own nuclear missile, Trident. Who, I wonder, are they aiming at? Osama bin Laden? You? Me? Joe Dokes? China? Paris? Who knows? What we do know is that this infantile insanity – the possession and threatened use of nuclear weapons – is at the heart of present American political philosophy. We must remind ourselves that the United States is on a permanent military footing and shows no sign of relaxing it.

Many thousands, if not millions, of people in the United States itself are demonstrably sickened, shamed and angered by their government's actions, but as things stand they are not a coherent political force – yet. But the anxiety, uncertainty and fear which we can see growing daily in the United States is unlikely to diminish.

I know that President Bush has many extremely competent speech writers but I would like to volunteer for the job myself. I propose the following short address which he can make on television to the nation. I see him grave, hair carefully combed, serious, winning, sincere, often beguiling, sometimes employing a wry smile, curiously attractive, a man's man.

'God is good. God is great. God is good. My God is good. Bin Laden's God is bad. His is a bad God. Saddam's God was bad, except he didn't have one. He was a barbarian. We are not barbarians. We don't chop people's heads off. We believe in freedom. So does God. I am not a barbarian. I am the democratically elected leader of a freedom-loving democracy. We are a compassionate society. We give compassionate electrocution and compassionate lethal injection. We are a great nation. I am not a dictator. He is. I am not a barbarian. He is. And he is. They all are. I possess moral authority. You see this fist? This is my moral authority. And don't you forget it.'

A writer's life is a highly vulnerable, almost naked activity. We don't have to weep about that. The writer makes his choice and is stuck with it. But it is true to say that you are open to all the winds, some of them icy indeed. You are out on your own, out on a limb. You find no shelter, no protection – unless you lie – in which case of course you have constructed your own protection and, it could be argued, become a politician.

I have referred to death quite a few times this evening. I shall now quote a poem of my own called 'Death'.

> *Where was the dead body found?*
> *Who found the dead body?*
> *Was the dead body dead when found?*
> *How was the dead body found?*
>
> *Who was the dead body?*
> *Who was the father or daughter or brother*
> *Or uncle or sister or mother or son*
> *Of the dead and abandoned body?*
>
> *Was the body dead when abandoned?*
> *Was the body abandoned?*
> *By whom had it been abandoned?*
>
> *Was the dead body naked or dressed for a journey?*
> *What made you declare the dead body dead?*
> *Did you declare the dead body dead?*
> *How well did you know the dead body?*
> *How did you know the dead body was dead?*
>
> *Did you wash the dead body?*
> *Did you close both its eyes?*
> *Did you bury the body?*

Did you leave it abandoned?
Did you kiss the dead body?

When we look into a mirror we think the image that confronts us is accurate. But move a millimetre and the image changes. We are actually looking at a never-ending range of reflections. But sometimes a writer has to smash the mirror – for it is on the other side of that mirror that the truth stares at us.

I believe that despite the enormous odds which exist, unflinching, unswerving, fierce intellectual determination, as citizens, to define the real truth of our lives and our societies is a crucial obligation which devolves upon us all. It is in fact mandatory.

If such a determination is not embodied in our political vision we have no hope of restoring what is so nearly lost to us – the dignity of man.

CHAPTER THREE

The Lighter Side

This chapter was added to capture the lighter side of President Bush's re-election that many publications from around the world effectively editorialized. There were also few interesting stories that were reported from around the world.

Honourable Sir, Congratulations

A Sri Lankan businessman was so confident President George W. Bush would be re-elected that he took out full page advertisements in all the island's leading newspapers to congratulate him in advance.

"Honourable Sir, Congratulations for your victory," read the advertisements on Monday Nov 1ˢᵗ 2004, prior to the election, with a picture of the grinning businessman next to a picture of Bush waving triumphantly.

"I love him... I think he is doing well. I think he is a great president," A.S.P. Liyanage, managing director of real-estate firm A.S.P. Constructions Private Ltd, had told the reporters.

Liyanage, who never set foot in the United States, spent one million rupees ($10,000) on the advertisements—around 10 years' salary for the average Sri Lankan.

"I want to encourage him and give my best wishes," he had added. "I think terrorism is a very, very big problem for the whole world. Somebody must take leadership for stopping terrorism... He is the leader, so he must do the leading."

With lots of difficulty, I was able to get a copy of the advertisement from Sri Lanka. We had to shrink it to scan it. But the image is visible enough to recognize the content.

An advertisement in a Sri Lankan newspaper

Migrate to Canada?

On November 6th 2004, AFP reported that many Americans were flirting with the idea of abandoning their homeland after President Bush's election win. It was reported that the number of U.S. citizens visiting Canada's main immigration Website shot up six-fold on November 3rd and the 4th.

In fact, Canadian immigration spokeswoman Maria Ladinardi had confirmed AFP that their Website did hit a new high on November 3rd, almost doubling the previous record high.

She added that on an average day some 20,000 people in the United States log on to the Website, http://www.cic.gc.ca, *a figure which rocketed to 115,016 on Wednesday, November 3rd. The number of U.S. visits settled down to 65,803 on Thursday, still well above the norm.*

Bush's victory sparked speculation that disconsolate Democrats and others might have decided to start a new life in Canada, a land that tilts more to the left than the United States. (It's interesting to note that Canadians elected a conservative government in 2006.)

Asked by a reporter whether an applicant would be looked upon more sympathetically if they claimed to be a sad Democrat seeking to escape four more years of Bush, Ladinardi replied, "There would be no weight given to statements of feelings."

I found some very interesting cartoons in Canadian newspapers and one fascinating opinion in a Caribbean newspaper that speculated on the idea of Bush-haters migrating to Canada.

The following opinion was published by the Trinidad and Tobago Express, *from the Caribbean. The author, Gwynne Dyer, is a Canadian journalist and author of more than six books including* Future: Tense: the Coming World Order.

—§—

The Divided States
Gwynne Dyer
Trinidad and Tobaco Express.

Looking at that extraordinary electoral map of the United States with all the liberal, quiche-eating, Kerry-supporting states of the northeast and the west coast coloured Democratic blue while the "heartland" and the south were solid Republican red, the solution to the problem suddenly occurred to me. "Blueland" should join Canada.

It is getting harder and harder for the two tribes of Americans to understand or even tolerate each other. Once again, as in 2000, the country is divided with almost mathematical precision into two halves, one of which adores President George W Bush while the other literally loathes him. And it goes far deeper than mere personalities or even the old left-right split; the clash now is about social norms and fundamental values on which few are willing to compromise. Opinions on the foreign issues that seemed to dominate the election-the war in Iraq and the "war on terror"-just mapped onto that existing cultural division. People who go to church regularly and oppose abortion and gay marriage were also far more likely to believe that US troops had found weapons of mass destruction in Iraq and that Saddam Hussein had somehow sponsored the terrorists of 9/11, so they voted for Mr Bush.

People who don't, didn't.

"Irreconcilable" is the word that springs to mind. Two separate populations have evolved in the United States, and they are increasingly unhappy even about living together. One sub-species, homo canadiensis, thinks medicare is a good idea, would rather send peacekeepers than bombers, and longs for the wimpy, wispy liberalism enjoyed by their Canadian neighbours to the north. The other breed, homo iraniensis, prefers the full-blooded religious certainties and the militant political slogans— "Death to... (fill in the blank)"—that play such a large and fulfilling part in Iranian public life. It is sheer cruelty to force these two populations to go on living together, especially since US political life has lost its centre and now pits these two irreconcilable opposites directly against each other in a winner-takes-all election every four years.

Since the pseudo-Iranians slightly outnumber the proto-Canadians, the obvious solution is for the latter group actually to go to Canada-and indeed, I have lost count of the number of American friends who have told me that if George W Bush wins again, they are going to move to Canada.

There are problems with this solution, however. A mass migration northwards would leave large chunks of the United States virtually empty, and the parts of Canada where people can live in any comfort are pretty full already. Besides, the winters up there really are fairly severe, and I'm not sure that Californians would be up to it. And then, looking at the two-colour map of the electoral outcome, the solution hit me. You don't have to move the people; just move the border.

It would all join up just fine: the parts of the US inhabited by homo canadiensis all lie along the Canadian border or next to other states that do (although the blue bit dangles down a long, long way in the case of the Washington-Oregon-California strip fondly known as the Left Coast).

True, the United States would lose its whole Pacific coast, but we could probably arrange for an American free port in, say, Tijuana. And lots of Canadians could move to a warmer clime without actually having to leave their country.

At the global level, everybody else would be quite happy with a bigger Canada and a smaller United States. That smaller US would have to pull in its horns a bit, as it would no longer have the resources to maintain military bases in every single country on the planet, but it would retain enough resources to invade a country every year or so, so it wouldn't suffer too badly from withdrawal symptoms. And the new Canadians would be free to have abortions, enter into gay marriages, do stem-cell research and engage in all other wickednesses that flourish in that bastion of corrupt and Godless liberalism. They could even speak French, if they wanted to.

No solution is perfect: there would be limp-wristed liberals trapped in the United States and God-fearing rednecks who suddenly found themselves in Canada, so some degree of population exchange would be necessary. It's even possible that a few right-wing bits of Canada-parts of Alberta, for example-might prefer to join the United States. But you can't make an omelette without breaking some eggs, and think how happy everybody will be when they are living exclusively among like-minded people.

Patrick Corrigan, The Toronto Star, Canada.

Nation's Poor Win Election for Nation's Rich

Remember the spectacular episodes of Survivor *in the islands of Vanuatu? How many of us knew that this tiny island in the South Pacific was eagerly watching the American presidential elections?*

I read one satire column in the Port Villa Presse, *one of the few newspapers published in Vanuatu. Although the satire piece was originally published by* The Onion *and was reprinted in* Port Villa Presse, *I thought it's worth sharing because Vanuatu was virtually unknown to many of us until the* Survivor *crew introduced it to Americans.*

Nations Poor Win Election For Nations Rich
By The Onion
Posted Tuesday, November 9, 2004

WASHINGTON, DC—The economically disadvantaged segment of the U.S. population provided the decisive factor in another presidential election last Tuesday, handing control of the government to the rich and powerful once again.

"The Republican party—the party of industrial mega-capitalists, corporate financiers, power brokers, and the moneyed elite—would like to thank the undereducated rural poor, the struggling blue-collar workers in Middle America, and the God-fearing underprivileged minorities who voted George W. Bush back into office," Karl Rove, senior advisor to Bush, told reporters at a press conference Monday. "You have selflessly sacrificed your well-being and voted against your own economic interest. For this, we humbly thank you."

Added Rove: "You have acted beyond the call of duty—or, for that matter, good sense."

According to Rove, the Republicans found strong support in non-urban areas populated by the people who would have benefited most from the lower-income tax cuts and social-service programs championed by Kerry. Regardless of their own interests, these citizens turned out in record numbers to elect conservatives into office at all levels of the government.

"My family's been suffering ever since I lost my job at the screen-door factory, and I haven't seen a doctor for well on four years now," said father of four Buddy Kaldrin of Eerie, CO. "Shit, I don't even remember what a dentist's chair looks like... Basically, I'd give up if it weren't for God's grace. So it's good to know we have a president who cares about religion, too."

Kaldrin added: "That's why I always vote straight-ticket Republican, just like my daddy did, before he lost the farm and shot himself in the head, and just like his daddy did, before he died of black-lung disease in the company coal mines."

Kaldrin was one of many who listed moral issues among their primary reasons for voting Republican.

"Our society is falling apart—our treasured values are under attack by terrorists," said Ellen Blaine of Givens, OH, a tiny rural farming community as likely to be attacked by terrorists as it is to be hit by a meteor. "We need someone with old-time morals in the White House. I may not have much of anything in this world, but at least I have my family."

Kerry Captures Bin Laden One Week Too Late.

"John Kerry is a flip-flopper," she continued. "I saw it on TV. Who knows what terrible things might've happened to my sons overseas if he'd been put in charge?"

Kerry supporters also turned out in large numbers this year, but they were outnumbered by those citizens who voted for Bush.

"The alliance between the tiny fraction at the top of the pyramid and the teeming masses of mouth-breathers at its enormous base has never been stronger," a triumphant Bush said. "We have an understanding, them and us. They help us stay rich, and in return, we help them stay poor. See? No matter what naysayers may think, the system works."

Added Bush: "God bless America's backwards hicks, lunchpail-toting blockheads, doddering elderly, and bumpity-car-driving Spanish-speakers."

CHAPTER FOUR

Osama helped Bush!

*W*ho could forget the October surprise? Osama bin Laden's October videotape gave plenty of fodder for columnists and cartoonists around the world and I was able to find many write-ups and caricatures related to this topic.

Will the Real President Please Stand Up?

The following opinion was published in the South African daily, The Star. *The author, Jovial Rantao, is the deputy editor of* The Star *and the editor of the* Sunday Independent, *both published from South Africa.*

Will the real president please stand up?
It is really public enemy Osama bin Laden who has won the
United States election.
November 5, 2004
By Jovial Rantao

So who really won the 2004 US elections? We know that it was not
John Kerry, after the US presidential hopeful conceded at 7pm on
Wednesday that his dream of becoming president of the most
powerful nation in the world had come crashing down.

We also know by now that George Bush has made his victory
speech, his first step towards his second term as president of the
United States.

However, did Kerry lose to George Bush, or did Osama bin
Laden win the election this week?

Sounds odd and cynical, you might say. How the hell can Osama
bin Laden — America's number one enemy — win a US election?

But think of it this way: going into the last weekend before the
poll, Bush and Kerry were in a dead heat.

"Too close to call," said the pundits.

"Prepare for the mother of all legal wrangles," warned others.

This was the scene until OBL entered the picture, in a dramatic
manner, on Saturday. In a move timed to influence the way in which
Americans voted, the feared leader of al-Qaeda had a few things to
say.

OBL attacked Bush, saying that his decision to sit in a Florida
classroom on the morning of the September 11 attacks had given the
suicide hijackers far more time to carry out their deadly missions.

"It never occurred to us that the commander-in-chief of the
American armed forces would leave 50 000 of his citizens in the two
towers to face these horrors alone ... " OBL said.

Never mind that the fact that OBL is still alive remains a major
indictment against Bush and his awesome military power. What was

important on Saturday October 30 were the words uttered by he with a goatee and a penchant for caves, bombs and human blood.

There is no doubt that OBL is US public enemy number one. There can also be no doubt that OBL is the subject of Bush's nightmares. This is the one single individual who had driven the naked, true meaning of fear into the hearts of Americans.

So when the OBL video hit television screens at the weekend, OBL drove the US voters — at least the undecided, mindful of his capabilities to sow terror and mayhem in any nation — into Bush's hands.

Kerry is a nice guy, but in Bush the Americans have someone who can at least stand up to OBL, or give an impression that he is doing so.

Even if he is economical with the truth, as has been the case in the war against terror, no one in the US really cares. As long as they have a belief that they can sleep easier at night. As long as Americans know that someone — Bush — is keeping an eye on the devil incarnate.

So Bush's tactic to play the politics of fear, to use his strategy of peace and security as a major weapon, has paid off, thanks to that timely intervention by OBL.

That timing is interesting, to say the least, given the revelation in the film Fahrenheit 9/11 on how Bush's administration intervened and gave OBL's family special dispensation to leave the US soon after the two hijacked planes were crashed into the World Trade Center's twin towers. Soon after that, the US government had grounded all planes.

A few months ago in Spain, questions were asked if al-Qaeda had won its first election. This was after bombs that exploded on rail tracks in Madrid, killing almost 200 train commuters, dramatically changed the voting trends.

That question has to arise now: Has al-Qaeda won its second major election and its first in the US?

I think it has.

Kerry did not lose because of his policies on homosexuals, guns and abortion. He lost because Americans felt that Bush was more equipped, as a cowboy, to take on the challenge laid out by OBL at the weekend.

And not only has OBL won, he has also set the US agenda for the next four years. So when Bush is inaugurated as the 44th president of the United States of America, look behind him and you will notice a shadow. It will be a long, lean figure, with flowing robes and a turban, long beard and might be carrying an AK-47 rifle in its hand.

That figure, I think, was the real victor — the real president of the US.

Perhaps it is time for a woman, a special woman, to take on OBL and succeed where men have failed. A special woman to bring back the American dream.

Perhaps that woman is Hillary Rodham Clinton.

She has four years in which to practise.

Hasan Bleibel, *Al-Mustakbal*, Beirut, Lebanon.

Julius Hansen, *Horsens Folkeblad*, Denmark.

GADO (Kenya) is the most Syndicated Political/Editorial cartoonist in the East and Central Africa.

CHAPTER FIVE

Faith-Based Presidency

*W*hen we analyze President Bush's re-election, no one can ignore the
God factor. The president's strong faith-based messages, focused on
*Christian values, played a vital role in the election. The rest of the world was very
keen on analyzing the so-called "faith-based presidency."*

*The following commentary is from one of the favorite holiday spots, the
Bahamas. The* Nassau Guardian, *one of the oldest newspapers in the Bahamas, ran this editorial.*

President Bush
Editorial – Nassau Guardian, Bahamas

The elections in the United States have now ended and George
Walker Bush has been returned as President of the United States of
America for a second term. He is the first of the four people who
have been president by virtue of winning the Electoral College but
losing the popular vote to win a second term. He also has the
distinction of receiving more votes than any other president in

history as well as he is the first president since his father George Herbert Walker Bush to receive more than 50 per cent of the popular vote.

With a majority of over three million I would say that he has a clear mandate to govern for the next four years. That fact not only scares the left wing in the United States but has Europeans scampering to figure out the rationale behind Americans returning George Bush to the presidency.

This has been fueled by the biased liberal press in the United States. If one were following the coverage on Tuesday like I was you would have been able to observe that there were long lines in most places of people anxious to cast their ballots. Indeed the exit polls showed a clear change was about to take place. It has always been stated that large voter turn out favoured the democrats.

Air America the liberal answer to conservative talk radio was championing these polls all day long as a sign that it would soon be President Kerry. I listened with glee and vowed to call in when what I saw as inevitable happened. I have tried but calling from The Bahamas is hard, not only to get through but a costly enterprise to endure the long waits on the telephone.

What they failed to realise is that exit polling is far from an accurate science and the television anchors seemed amazed all night that they were continuously off base. Another factor that the Democrats failed to take into account is that many people are now seeking a higher ground.

They crave a higher moral plateau be that through Christianity or what ever means the vote demonstrates that the populace want and expect people to be held more accountable. The liberals have for so long sought to find built-in excuses for everything and the people are just tired of it.

What ever happened to old fashioned personal accountability? If you did the crime you did the time. Not any more. How often these days when watching American news do you hear excuses such as, he did that because he came from a single parent home, he lacked male guidance, he grew up in the projects, his family was dysfunctional and it goes on and on.

Another facet was that Democrats refuse to seek out the church vote. Yes they seek the black church vote because it is felt that as the blacks hate the Republicans in any event that to canvass them would off set their shortfalls. What this election showed was that the black church vote itself is now making the switch.

The Republicans have made it a central issue to appeal to the moral fiber of America and even though the black vote by and large is Democrat with the televangelist explosion many blacks are realising that they have more in common with the Republicans when it comes to values than they do the Democrats.

Thus the blacks that left the Republican fold in droves during the Reagan years because the Republicans realised at the time that they didn't need to cater to them and still maintain power are now finding a home in the same party that discarded them based simply on shared moral values.

Let's not be mistaken, President Bush only polled a little over nine per cent of the black vote but that figure is significantly higher than it used to be.

The Democrats need to stop telling people what they think they want and listen to what the people are actually saying. The problem I always had with liberals is that for all the good they attempt to do, they do so for the wrong reasons. That is they seek to look back and say look what we did to better your lives. That was the problem with the welfare system when controlled by the liberals as there was never a cut off point and thus never an incentive for the recipient to do for themselves and therefore feel that sense of pride that only comes when you have achieved something for yourself.

If you are going to give me something with no strings attached and then seek to buy my vote each time by increasing what I receive then you are going to get many people to vote for you, especially when you can point to someone and call them the big bad wolf because they want to take that support system away. However after welfare reform many of the abusers of the system had no choice but to do for themselves as there was a now termination point. For all the hoopla that this was going to be the ruining of the nation and it showed just how little the Republicans cared for the poor, the shift produced seems to be only in what people now expect and want. They want a level playing field where there are systems of values and core beliefs.

As for us in The Bahamas we will see what the election means. Congratulations President Bush.

A Big Win for Bush

The following opinion is from the Manila Bulletin, *published in the Philippines, a country with a strong Christian population.*

A big win for Bush
Manila Bulletin
Beth Day Romulo

ALL during this fall election season, we were deluged with polls, predictions, opinions from political pundits that this would be one of the closest presidential races in the American history. And it was supposedly neck-and neck up to the final showdown, with only two points separating the contestants in the electoral college, when Ohio, with its 20 electoral votes fell to the President and the race was over. Kerry gracefully conceded without putting the country through the agony of a contested outcome. But the big surprise was that President Bush got an astonishing three million vote lead in the popular vote — far more than in his first election, four years ago.

So what went wrong? Sifting through the analyses and predictions covering the bitterly contested campaign, I found only one report that predicted what really happened, an article in the NY Times magazine called the "Faith-Based Presidency" in which the author Ron Suskind makes the point that Kerry was not reaching the very people he sought to represent: Middle America. One assumption is that people trusted Bush more than Kerry on the security issue. But what appears equally, if not more, important, is the "moral" issue. 42 percent of Americans are evangelical ("born again") Christians. They abhor gay marriage, liberal politicians, and apparently care little about the environment or what happens overseas. They are simply not concerned with internationalism and foreign policy. While the Kerry people did well in sophisticated urban areas, they didn't catch fire in the heartland of America, where liberals are viewed with suspicion as elitists from the east coast. The fact that America has pursued a unilateral course abroad which antagonizes former allies apparently is of little concern. It's the, "us against them" mentality in which America is viewed, morally, as the leader of the world whose duty it is to spread democracy and freedom and faith. While Kerry talked "issues," Bush preached "moral" values.

Bush "appears to believe he's on a mission from God" as one aide put it, and this sort of certainty is reassuring to religious Americans. Visiting America, one senses an air of gloom and fear in America today that this assurance of the president's plays into. America's mainland was never attacked before 9/11 (the closest was the Aleutian Islands in World War II) and Americans are fearful of attack in a way they have never been before. Bush presents himself as a strong leader, who can handle homeland security, which Senator Kerry did not convey strongly enough. But moral values, even more than security fears seems to have been a major factor among the huge turnout of voters — which was supposed to have gone in Mr. Kerry's favor. Gay marriage, the appointment of a new conservative Supreme Court justice, the privatization of social security, opening up environmentally protected lands for oil exploration – all these played to the religious right and middle America.

Instead of the dead-heat race they anticipated, the election was as a disaster for the Democrats. They not only lost the presidency but also seats in Congress and, most importantly, their effective minority leader, Senator Tom Daschle. The only important Democratic victory was the election of the Democratic convention star, their keynote speaker Barack Obama, as senator from Illinois, who will be the only African-American in the Senate.

So far as Asia is concerned, we can expect continuity of current policies, barring major changes in the Cabinet.

It is the Republican party itself that bears close watching. They have kept the presidency. They have added seats in both the Senate and the House. But the party itself is split on many of the issues on the president's agenda. A former Reagan aide, Bruce Bartlett, predicted that if Bush stayed on the job, "there will be a civil war within the Republican Party."

Welcome Back, Mr. Bush

The following opinion is from a publication called the Accra-Mail, *from Ghana. Although the article focuses more on reaching out to the rest of the world, the writer claims that God—one of the Gs (God, Gay, and Gun) that Bush supposedly used effectively to win the election.*

Welcome back, Mr. Bush...
Accra Mail - Ghana
Friday, November 05, 2004

We wish to take this opportunity to congratulate US President George Bush for his re-election to the White House for a second term. It was a hard fought political battle between him and his Democratic opponent, the outcome of which clearly showed Mr. Bush as the choice of the American people.

Interestingly, world opinion outside the US favoured a Kerry win and this to us is a clear message to Mr. Bush that his second term's agenda would have to take the whole world on board.

Some Americans may argue that the rest of us do not really matter in this purely American affair, but there we believe they would be wrong. The US needs the rest of the world and the world equally needs US science, technology, innovation and money.

The US is one country that has a little bit of every country and that is why it is truly the melting pot of world cultures. Any insularity in foreign policy naturally also creates tensions between America and the rest of the world.

We therefore do not wish to see Mr. Bush's re-election as a victory for any one particular group but as a victory for the entire US and signals the coming together of the international community to confront the many challenges facing mankind.

A commentator on an international radio station remarked that President Bush effectively tapped into the three Gs (God, Guns and Gays) to win the election. He may or he may not have benefited from these Gs, but what remains to be done is for Bush to make peace with the rest of the world during this second term.

Too many fences were torn down during his first term. To continue with the view that the rest of the world that does not go along with US foreign policy is irrelevant would mean that the war on terrorism would take a much longer time to win — that is if it can be won at all.

We hope Mr. Bush would succeed in dispelling all those doubts that made the rest of the world wish he had lost the elections to Kerry and really become the undisputed leader of the modern world.

Welcome back, Mr. President and good luck in your second term.

Now the Fun Really Begins!

The following column, which again looks at the faith-based theories, was written by a popular Jamaican columnist, Keeble McFarlen, and was published in the Jamaica Observer.

Now the fun really begins!
Keeble McFarlen
Saturday, November 06, 2004

Now that the Bushling has renewed his lease on the White House for another four years, the world is in for the wildest roller-coaster ride it can imagine.

Regrettably, regime change did not take place in Washington, which sees itself as the most important city on the face of the Earth since civilisation began. In fact, what happened last Tuesday was a cementing of simplistic, neo-conservative, ultra right-wing, religious zealotry under the guise of politics.

Afrikaans, the language of the conservative old Dutch settlers who colonised South Africa three and a half centuries ago, has two words which neatly describe the two factions which have been going at each other ever since the United States Supreme Court awarded George Bush II the White House four years ago.

Those words are verkrampte, which describes people with an extremely limited, narrow-minded view of the world; and verligte, which means "enlightened", "open-minded", "progressive".

This week, the verkramptes won, and will continue to try to reshape the world according to their severely constrained attitudes toward everything: from what should be taught in school to the kind of research the government should not pay for.

In his victory speech, Bush vowed to reach out to those who did not vote for him, but taken in the context of his behaviour over the past four years, especially during the election campaign, this sounds more than a bit hollow.

In fact, he won largely because his right-hand political operative Karl Rove, master of back-alley fighting and dirty tricks, targeted the Bible-belt Americans who did not vote on the last occasion.

They form the bedrock of Bush's support, and Rove made sure his boss played to that crowd.

The moralistic appeal wasn't apparent to the chattering classes in the media and the fancy salons of the big cities, and during the Republican convention Rove "low-keyed" it to the point where you could detect it only by attending the various committee and delegate meetings scattered throughout the convention.

The keynote speeches skirted those themes and addressed the wider audience outside the convention through television. But it did not go unnoticed that Bush's father — a former president and long-serving party mogul — was not invited to speak or even appear for a photo-op at the shindig in New York.

During the campaign, though, Bush played the piety card as he stumped the country, addressing carefully assembled crowds packed with the faithful and excluding anyone who showed the slightest sign of dissidence, such as a T-shirt slogan.

He addressed all the hot-button issues for those crowds — abortion; homosexuality and especially the desire of many to be granted the legal right to marry; control of firearms; the fight against terrorism; and above all, his hinting that he has a direct pipeline to the Almighty.

Don't forget that very early in his first term Bush made the Centres for Disease Control pull from their website and other informational materials all references to the use of condoms as one of the tools to fight AIDS, and also cut off any financial support to international organisations fighting the disease if they didn't stick to the script that abstinence is the only proper way to deal with AIDS.

On the legal front, Bush has been packing lower— and middle-level federal courts with some of the most Neanderthal judges he could find, and has the opportunity to do the same for the nine-member Supreme Court, up to four of whose members are due for retirement, either by way of illness or fatigue.

You can bet he'll name the most reactionary types available, and with the Republicans in complete control of the House of Representatives and the Senate, it will be very difficult to stop the progress of the elephantine steam-roller as it paves the way for overturning laws the zealots don't like, such as Roe vs. Wade, which allows a woman to have an abortion.

We all remember, of course, that when the terrorists flew those aeroplanes into the towers in New York, just about everyone of significance in the world gave their support when the US struck out against Afghanistan, which was harbouring Osama bin Laden. But very soon Bush and his vengeful minions took their eye off the target and shifted instead to Saddam Hussein, who had nothing to do with 9/11.

He ignored the same people who applauded when he went after al-Qaeda and who now expressed misgivings about the relevance of Iraq. Some of us remember the underlying emotional reason, as Bush expressed a couple of years ago: "He tried to kill muh daddy." Not to mention the huge pool of oil sitting under the parched sands of Iraq, barely tapped.

Then there's that simplistic view that you can plant democracy in infertile soil such as you find in an old, traditionalist society like Iraq, and expect it to sprout into something solid in a short while. Unfortunately, Iraq has become Bush's Tar Baby, from which he cannot disengage, even though Iraqis now can't stand the presence of the Americans and their allies.

Going into the war, he had no plan of how to get out, and, like Vietnam a generation ago, this one promises to grow into an open, running sore, oozing lives and resources long after Bush's second lease on the White House expires. The next president will have to clean up that mess. (Remember what Vietnam did to Lyndon Johnson?) And Bush has dusted off and updated an old American concept of manifest destiny, and has come out with a policy of preventive deterrence — the US can attack any country it wants to, if it feels that that country may possibly be thinking about attacking it, or even has the potential capacity to do so.

Now, I don't for one minute think they'll invade North Korea, since even though it is an extremely impoverished country, it still possesses sharp and solid teeth, some of them nuclear ("nucular", in Bush-talk), and appears quite willing to use them.

Duppy, indeed, knows who to frighten.

However, you can see the possibility of Bush striking at a country close by, not because it poses a military or economic threat to the US, but because it is so different from what Bush thinks a country should be like, and because it has defied all efforts to toe any line drawn by Washington, the Europeans or anybody else.

The Cubans would be the least surprised of all if Bush were to launch such an attack on them, especially since the Bush League has been doing the spade-work.

A document prepared for Secretary of State Colin Powell lays out scenarios and possible plans for what Washington deems to be the restoration of democracy to that stubborn and independent-minded island and its obstinate and annoyingly long-lived leader.

Some people suggest that Castro and his associates are showing paranoia when they mount military and civil-defence exercises to repel possible attacks by the US. But they know from four decades of experience that even paranoiacs have enemies.

—§—

CHAPTER SIX

The Israel Factor

*T*his book would not be complete if I ignored the reaction from Israel. After all, Israel is at the center on all of the issues that have been discussed so far. So what do Israelis think about America? What did they write about American voters? What advice do they have for the Jewish voters in the U.S.?*

With much difficulty I found the following two opinions from two distinguished publications in Israel.

—§—

God Fearing or Fearing God

The following piece was published by the Maariv International, Israel. The author, Jonathan Rosenblum, is the director of Jewish Media Resources, a leading media organization dedicated to furthering an understanding of Torah Judaism. Jewish Media Resources works with journalists by providing information and insights about the Orthodox Jewish community in Israel and access to leading figures within the community. Mr. Rosenblum also serves as an English language spokesman for the Orthodox Jewish community with foreign journalists.

God fearing or fearing God
Secular Jews have gone from no longer being God fearing to actively fearing God.
Jonathan Rosenblum

The October 13 JTA carried three items that reveal a great deal about the state of American Jewry. The first concerns a new cartoon posted on the website of the National Jewish Democratic Council. It features a character named "Bubbie," who pounds various Republican luminaries into unconsciousness with her handbag. In one scene, Bush advisor Karl Rove is seen addressing a group of Republican faithful, all dressed in red cassocks (suggestive of the white robes worn at Ku Klux Klan meetings) from a pulpit adorned with a crucifix.

One wonders about the wisdom of Jews, who constitute 2% (and shrinking) of the American population, expressing their contempt for Christians, even devout ones, by portraying them as dangerous religious fanatics.

The cartoon, however, nicely captures the horror many American Jews feel towards Christians, particularly evangelical Christians. Ninety-five per cent of evangelicals, incidentally, say that support for Israel is the most important issue for them in the upcoming presidential election (the second JTA item), as opposed to only 15% of American Jews who list Israel as among their top three concerns. It would seem that American Jews have fewer problems with the Presbyterians, who, like them, have reduced religion to "good deeds" such as boycotting Israel.

Eli Valley, the author of a recent Jerusalem Post piece, who works for Jewish philanthropist Michael Steinhardt, warns that President Bush's evangelical supporters are bent on "converting the Jews and ending the Jewish religion." Given the phenomenal success of American Jews themselves in ending the Jewish religion through intermarriage and assimilation it is unclear why the evangelicals should cause shudders.

The horror of evangelicals easily morphs into contempt for religion altogether, and Christian-phobia into God-phobia. The most frightening thing about George W. Bush, in Valley's view, is that "he has made no secret of his religious devotion." Religious people are portrayed as incapable of rational thought, and Bush's "faith-based-reasoning" contrasted to Kerry's "fact-based" approach. For good measure, Valley implies, that Bush may actually court nuclear disaster out of a longing for Apocalypse. (Shades of Matti Golan's "Atom.")

Cameron Kerry, a Reform convert, recently tried to sell his brother's candidacy to a group of Orthodox Jews on the grounds that his brother would never appoint an Attorney-General who begins his work day with prayer like John Ashcroft. That line had no doubt proven a sure winner with secular Jewish groups. How was the hapless Kerry to know that Orthodox Jews begin and end their day the same way.

Out of fear of aiding and abetting religion, major American Jewish groups, including the Reform movement, consistently adopt the most extreme positions on separation of state and religion. Noted constitutional scholar Nathan Lewin has quipped that the only Wall at which American Jewry worships is the wall of separation between state and religion. As an example (JTA item 3), the Reform movement recently advised its congregations against accepting any Homeland Security funds for guarding their temples and schools from terrorist attack, despite the obvious appeal of Jewish institutions for Islamic terrorists.

The consequence of this disdain and scoffing at people of religious faith and the determination to keep any taint of religion out of the public square is to convince Jewish kids that belief in G-d – and certainly the view that any consequences might flow from that belief – is simply not intellectually serious. And it is that attitude that has brought American Jewry to the edge of extinction.

Will Jews Still Vote like Puerto Ricans?

Tom Gross is a former Jerusalem correspondent for the Sunday Telegraph *of* London. *The following comment first appeared in the* Jerusalem Post, *and the version reprinted here is a longer version of the article that appeared at* Israel Insider *(http://www.israelinsider.com).*

Tom was kind enough to provide me with an update to his original piece and asked me to include the introduction.

INTRODUCTION

This comment piece, analyzing Jewish voting intentions, was published in The Jerusalem Post the day before the November 2, 2004 US presidential election. (It was also reprinted on the day of the election on a number of Israeli and other websites.)

The article was not meant to be taken as an endorsement of either presidential candidate. It simply drew attention to an aspect of the 2004 U.S. election – regarded by many analysts as a "foreign policy election" – which might reasonably be considered puzzling. Why did so few Jews say they would vote for George W. Bush, even though possibly no president in history has been more favorably disposed to Jewish concerns, and even though it was also in the economic interest of many Jews to vote for him.

Bush, as we know, went on to win re-election with a strong popular mandate. Yet, US Jews remained one of the groups most supportive of his Democrat opponent, John Kerry, even though Kerry had been lukewarm on Israel, and had spoken of Yasser Arafat a "statesman."

In November 2004, a higher proportion of Hispanics, homosexuals, Arab-Americans and other minority groups, voted for Bush than US Jews did. And when one considers that the hundreds of thousands of American Jews from the former Soviet Union voted overwhelmingly for Bush, the anti-Bush vote among other American Jews was even more lopsided.

— Tom Gross

THE ARTICLE

Puerto Ricans have moved on. Why not Jews?

US presidential voting habits remain a puzzle.

By Tom Gross

November 1, 2004

The Jerusalem Post (Opinion Page)

Once upon a time most American Jews were underprivileged, and most of them voted Democrat. Then their circumstances changed, but their political allegiances remained unaltered. Around 30 or 40 years ago there was a joke which said that American Jews live like Episcopalians (i.e. relatively rich, privileged people) but vote like Puerto Ricans.

The remark was a bit racist, perhaps, but it was essentially true. Everyone knew what it meant. Only it is not true anymore. Puerto Ricans, like other Hispanics, have moved on. They now vote in a pluralistic way in accordance with their developing economic interests, ethnic concerns and what they think is good for America. In 2000 the Hispanic vote for George W Bush was more than 50 percent greater than the Jewish vote.

This year American Jews remain as intransigent as ever. Jews, more than almost any other group in the US, are set to vote against Bush by large margins.

Polls indicate that 69 percent of Jews will vote Kerry tomorrow, and only 24 percent for Bush. And 3 percent will vote for Ralph Nader, the strongly anti-Israel independent candidate of Arab descent who according to polls commands less than half that support among non-Jewish Americans.

Yet the situation is even more lopsided than it first appears: What the over-all figure doesn't take into account is that the hundreds of thousands of American Jews from the former Soviet Union – who know a thing of two about oppression, terrorism, anti-Semitism and the meaning of freedom – are overwhelmingly pro-Bush. Only 14 percent say they will back Kerry.

THE RIGHT NOT TO GET YOUR HEAD CHOPPED OFF.

Naturally, many Jews will vote on issues completely unrelated to foreign policy or their own economic status – issues of social justice, abortion, gay rights and so on. But much more than usual, this is a foreign policy election. At the moment the right not to get your head chopped off seems more important than that of, say, gay marriage.

According to the polls, other Americans recognize this, and given the rise in global anti-Semitism (a hatred directed at America's Jews as much as any others) foreign policy concerns should be of exceptional importance to Jews. If they haven't read Bin Laden's key 1998 text, "Jihad against Jews and Crusaders," issued by The World Islamic Front, they should. Ignoring it is as foolish as it would have been to ignore Mein Kampf.

In the last four years Jews have been specifically targeted in terror attacks in Casablanca, Djerba, Kenya, Istanbul, the Sinai, and Los Angeles, among other places. Even those behind the Madrid bombs say they were looking to bomb Spain's (very few) Jewish targets. Daniel Pearl was killed as a Jew.

And – yes – there is 9/11 too. For many in the Moslem world are convinced that when al Qaeda chose the Twin Towers as their target, it was because in their anti-Semitic world view, Jews control American finance: they saw the Towers as a Jewish target, and aimed to kill as many Jews as possible.

Support for Israel is "a very important factor" in their lives, say 74 percent of American Jews. Bush is generally regarded as not only the most pro-Israel president ever, but probably the most pro-Jewish one as well. His signing last month of the Global Anti-Semitism Awareness Act, requiring the State Department to monitor anti-Semitic abuses around the world, is only the latest example of this. In explaining their support for this act, leading Republicans Jack Kemp and Jeanne Kirkpatrick, said anti-Semitism is bad not only for Jews, but "a measure of the democratic instability of other countries."

PALESTINIAN-AMERICANS FOR BUSH

Yet, even though Kerry has called Yasser Arafat "a statesman," has criticized Israel's security fence as a "barrier to peace," and has not noticeably protested any U.N. actions attacking Israel, according to polls more Jews may well vote Kerry than Palestinian-Americans will.

When Bush stood for president four years ago, there was little to indicate that he would grasp the necessity for reform in the Arab world – as an American interest, an Israeli interest, and most importantly as an Arab interest. It is clear that he does now.

It should be equally clear that many of the Clinton administration's policies were unwise not only in terms of American national interest but also from a humanitarian viewpoint – in particular the extraordinary appeasement of Arafat and the red-carpet treatment given to him while he violated every single one of the Oslo accords, the failure to take the al Qaeda threat seriously, and the failure to exert any kind of meaningful pressure on regimes in Riyadh, Damascus and elsewhere.

Yet there is every indication that the foreign policy team Kerry would assemble, should he win, would comprise many of the same people who made such glaring mistakes in the 1990s.

This is why some major Jewish Democratic Party figures, such as former New York mayor Ed Koch, have endorsed Bush. Why Al Gore's running mate Joe Lieberman hinted last month that Bush might be better for Israel. Why the leading liberal journalist Martin Peretz wrote last week, "A President Kerry would be a disaster for Israel."

Whereas non-Jewish Americans I have spoken to in recent months are split roughly 50-50 in their voting preferences, as one might expect given the neck and neck polls, almost all my Jewish American friends are backing Kerry.

THE BIGGEST RETURN OF REFUGEES IN HISTORY.

Why? I asked an American Jewish friend who lives in the London, last month. "Because Kerry is for human rights," was the answer. Apparently he didn't know until I told him that it was Bush who had made possible one of the biggest repatriations of refugees in history (over three million Afghans have returned home thanks to his policies) or that the Taliban regime that Bush removed crushed homosexuals to death as a matter of policy. Nor was he aware of how many people had died under Saddam.

What could be more liberal, indeed more radical than that? This is among the reasons why "The American Conservative" magazine last week endorsed Kerry, but Christopher Hitchens, writing in America's leading left-wing magazine, The Nation, endorsed Bush. Hitchens (correctly) calls this "a single-issue election and seems to imply that in their hearts, liberals and leftists know Bush's foreign policies are right. "Do you know anybody who really, deeply wishes that Carter had been re-elected, or that Dukakis had won?"

As for my Arab friends, there is already much talk about the fact that Kerry is "a Jew" (no matter that he is in fact a Catholic of part-Jewish origin) and this, they say, should be highlighted if he supports Israel.

We are likely to hear much more about this in future if he becomes president. Last week in Prague, the archivist of the Czech Jewish Federation showed me the "transportation certificates" for the brother and sister of Kerry's grandmother Ida: Otto Lowy, who died in Terezin, and Jenny Lowy, who was taken on from Terezin to Treblinka where she was gassed.

Indeed many Jews seem unperturbed that Kerry has long presented himself, for the purpose of the Massachusetts vote, as a Catholic of presumably Irish origins, and that for years even after he was aware of them, concealed his Jewish origins and the fact that his grandfather changed his name from Kohn (a derivation of Cohen) to Kerry. Someone who is evasive about such an important matter doesn't inspire much trust in general. (Even Al-Riyadh, a Saudi government daily, criticized him last month for concealing his Jewish roots.)

Given past voting habits and domestic concerns, one would not, perhaps, expect Jews to vote overwhelmingly for Bush. But that in 2004 so many are opposed so violently – often hysterically – to a leader who has proved a good friend, is puzzling.

CHAPTER SEVEN

Change or No Change?

*W*hile *Americans thought that the rest of the world almost whole-heartedly preferred John Kerry to be the president, some of the analysis from the Arab world claimed that neither candidate could have brought any positive changes to their part of the world. It was enlightening to see how these countries compared the candidates.*

The following piece was published by Cairolive.com, *an online news source operating in Egypt.*

Rocks in a Candy Shop

Egyptians may not like Kerry...
but they really hate Bush
by Tarek Atia
Cairolive.com

There is a recurring theme in US presidential politics, at least from an Arab point of view. And it goes like this: while Israel is in a candy shop, choosing between a lollipop and gum, each sweeter than the other, Arabs are like Charlie Brown at Halloween—their trick or treat bag is full of rocks.

It's hard, after all, to choose between two candidates who appear little better than each other on issues of most concern to Arabs. "Kerry seems more rational," was a typical response to a straw poll conducted by Egyptian newspaper Al-Ahram Weekly of 100 randomly picked Egyptians—as well as 10 prominent public figures—regarding how they would vote and why. "He seems less dangerous than Bush." The key word, in both sentiments, is "seems", since no one knows for sure.

Most respondents were much clearer on the way they felt about Bush. "I hate Bush because we know he hates our guts," was retired re-insurance executive Fathi Hamam's blunt response. The vast majority of those polled — 90 per cent or so—echoed his sentiments. "Saying the word 'crusade' made him look like a crusader," Hamam explained. "If there is even a one per cent chance that Kerry will be different, then we should try him."

The majority of respondents to the poll — 51 per cent—would vote for Kerry, given the chance. A significant 32 per cent chose neither. Bush got only 12 per cent of the votes, while five per cent chose Ralph Nader.

That same dynamic seems to govern the way most of the world is watching what appear to be the most anticipated elections in recent US history. Surveys are being conducted everywhere. A British paper even tried to influence voters in Ohio, with often disastrously hilarious results.

The world is monitoring the US elections as if they were their own, and with good reason; rarely has the identity of the man occupying the White House had such global relevance. The events of the last four years, under George W Bush, have conspired to make that a virtually irrefutable fact.

Outside observers might question the validity of asking people who have little or no say in their own domestic politics to comment on elections in "a galaxy far, far away". Egyptians, after all, choose their president by referendum—by saying yes or no to just one candidate.

But world citizens have a clear stake in who heads the sole global super power. After all, according to Gamil Mattar, director of the Arab Centre for Development and Futuristic Research, "what happens in the US today has a direct effect on the whole world, and it will stay that way until God knows when."

In the Arab world, as was made clear by the survey, as well as by similar experiments on radio, TV, and in other media outlets, politics is local. "Bush has been treating the Arab world as if it were an American state," one caller told Negoum FM. That feeling is the driving force behind most people's desire to have "anyone but Bush" sitting behind the Oval Office desk. "Let's find out what Kerry has in store for our region," medical student Mohamed Adel told the Weekly.

Many respondents were hyper-aware of the fact that whoever governs America is bound to be pro-Israeli. "I see Sharon in both," said Hoda Amer, the director of the People's Assembly media department. "Bush is Kerry and Kerry is Bush. They will both be controlled by Israel," was teacher Said Morsi's response.

Some, like banker Hussein El-Sherif, had a more nuanced view. "Because he cannot run for a third term, and therefore does not have to adopt policies that satisfy the Jewish lobby, Bush may think about improving his policies towards the Arab region before leaving office for good."

Political analyst Osama El-Ghazali Harb was also optimistic about Bush learning from "experience, which will make him wiser". In any case, Harb, the editor of Al-Ahram's Al-Siyassa Al-Dawlia (International Politics) quarterly, said the US is "an institutional state, not one that is purely governed by its presidents."

Bush's wars on Afghanistan, terror and Iraq have meant that many don't see it that way. Housewife Nermeen Abdel-Meguid said that, "US elections are a stage-play the end of which is known. Bush and Kerry are two sides of one coin. It's all fake and we, the Arabs, will lose in both cases."

Neither Bush nor Kerry is "up to the standard one would expect of a US president", says Mustafa El-Feki, chairman of parliament's foreign affairs committee, even as he asserted that Kerry would be the better choice.

TV technician Ahmed Abdel-Hamid was more blunt, about Bush at least, calling him "a mentally-backward barbarian and thug". In fact, people of all social classes and occupations, from butchers to university lecturers, tended to feel the same way about Bush and his Likudist, neo-con gang of advisors. That, and the perception that Republicans were more likely to be anti-Arab than Democrats, propelled many into choosing Kerry — albeit unenthusiastically. Student Mo'men Mohamed said the Massachusetts senator would only provide "different pretexts for wars and the occupation of weak countries".

Interestingly, Essam El-Erian, a leading member of the outlawed Muslim Brotherhood—although ultimately opting for Kerry — gave Bush credit for "forcing Arab governments onto the road for change".

One of the potential beneficiaries of that new dynamic—the just licensed El-Ghad (Tomorrow) party's secretary-general Mona Makram Ebeid, would still opt for Kerry since "he wants to have positive relations with the rest of the world". In any case, Ebeid said, "having a new US president would be a psychological change for the entire world, and it might defuse the unbearable tension that currently exists".

Always adept at breaking tension with a joke or two, some respondents exhibited Egyptians' sense of humour in full force: "I have become very used to both Bush and his father. I can't imagine a US president that doesn't have Bush as a family name," said gift shop owner Safia El-Said. Teaching assistant Mohamed Selim suggested a rather unlikely write-in candidate—Hizbullah's Hassan Nasrallah.

The black and white world Bush has catalysed may work in Kerry's favour come 2 November. Then again, there are those in the Arab world who appear to share the sentiments of janitor Abdel-Fatah Ismail, who told us "the devil we know is better than the devil we don't. You never know what Kerry is hiding up his sleeve."

For this part of the world, however, housewife Amani Mahmoud's sentiment may be the most relevant for now—"Arabs should not get their hopes up with this election."

VAL, of VIETBAO.com, a Vietnam news portal.

Repairing the Relations

The following column was published by the Manila Bulletin *in the Philippines soon after President Bush won his second term. Although the piece is somewhat Filipino specific, it claims that Kerry had an Atlantic bias. The author, Edgardo Angara, is a senator in the Philippines.*

Repairing the Relations
By: Sen. Edgardo Angara
Philippines

For a while, we had treaded on jittery grounds in our own fight against terror when we displeased America and the Coalition of the Willing in saving the life of Angelo de la Cruz. But with the second term win by President George W. Bush, we have been given an opportune time to repair and strengthen our relations with the United States.

A Republican win may be good for the Philippines. US Republican Presidents have always looked more kindly towards our country. In fact, two Republican Presidents – Dwight Eisenhower and George W. Bush – have traveled to the country to address the joint sessions of the Philippine Congress.

The Philippines, too, has had a deep historical affinity with the US Republican government. The Republicans tended to be more friendly to the Filipinos. They have always shown a keen interest in our welfare and development.

Our Filipino World War II veterans, for example, are very grateful to the former President George Bush, the elder, under whose term their plight was given much-needed attention. Some even chose to become American citizens under the Immigration Act of 1990 and live in the United States. Today, in their old age, hundreds of them are enjoying supplemental security income as well as medical care and other benefits.

The Democrats, on the other hand, have always been Eurocentric. Their attention is more focused on the Atlantic than the Pacific.

I personally know Senator John Kerry and have met him on several occasions. The first time was when he was an observer, along with Sen. Richard Lugar, during the snap elections in 1985. We met again during the state visit of then President Aquino to the United States. I found him extremely intelligent. But like most of his fellow Democrats, he is more interested in Atlantic affairs.

As for President Bush, his administration can be expected to be a more sympathetic and helpful presidency following the Republican tradition.

The next four years under President Bush is hoped to bring about better US-Philippine relations. There may be no other time when both countries could need each other in many areas, including the fight against terrorism.

The geopolitical situation in this part of the world requires fostering and the cultivation of relations for the two countries' mutual benefit.

Patrick Chappatte, *International Herald Tribune.*

No Guarantee Kerry would Love Zimbabwe

The following article is from the troubled Zimbabwe. Daily News, *the publication that ran this piece, was shut down in 2005 when armed policemen raided the newspaper and ordered the staff to leave its offices. The closure of the* Daily News *marked the first time since the 1960s that a newspaper had been banned in Zimbabwe.*

On the 16th and 17th of September 2005, police confiscated computers and other equipment from the offices of the newspaper. Over one hundred pro-democracy activists protesting the closure of the paper were also arrested. Since its launch in 1999, the Daily News *has been the target of two bomb attacks, and several of its journalists, including the former editor-in-chief Geoffrey Nyarota, have been arrested repeatedly.*

No guarantee Kerry would love Zimbabwe
Date: 27-Oct, 2004
By Munodii Kunzwa

Most politically savvy Africans don't hold out much hope that United States foreign policy would undergo a sea-change after next week's presidential election.

American voters are influenced more by domestic policies than by such esoteric foreign concerns as the political skullduggery in the Masvingo South parliamentary constituency in Zimbabwe.

But Iraq is a domestic as well as a foreign policy issue. George W. Bush's chances of winning or losing depend on Iraq.

If the Americans think he has done a good job there - never mind throwing more Americans out of employment than any other president in a long time - then they will vote for him.

If they believe this is the biggest Bush blunder since his father threw up all over a Japanese prime minister, then he is sunk. But for Zimbabwe, a Bush defeat might not necessarily herald a change in the US view of what Robert Mugabe has done to and with his country.

Or its global significance: a pariah state, the target of the US Zimbabwe Democracy and Economic Recovery Act, suspended from the Commonwealth, the target of "smart" and other not-so-smart sanctions by the European Union and others.

All this, not because Zimbabwe helped train Al Qaeda terrorists, or banned the sale of Coca-Cola, Superman comics and Mother's Apple Pie, but because it played dirty pool in its own presidential election.

By all estimates, the US has lost nothing because of the strained relations with Zimbabwe. Admittedly, a big minus might be the spectacle of the leader of the world's most powerful nation being called dirty names by what some Americans might call a two-bit African dictator — on American soil.

Mugabe did that at the United Nations General Assembly last month, calling Bush Blair's sidekick or disciple or poodle or words to that effect. US law could not touch him for, in fact, he was not on American soil but on "world" soil.

There is no need to speculate on what would happen to a Zimbabwean calling Mugabe dirty names on his home soil. But apart from that, it is Zimbabwe which has lost out.

Its relations with the rest of the world are not exactly what even the most generous commentator would describe as "a house on fire", or going "swimmingly".

The economy is being buffeted from all sides as a result of this alienation and the call for entrepreneurs "to go East" has not proved attractive enough to compensate for the loss of trade with the West.

John Kerry, the democratic Party's candidate, is the more idealistic of the two men. Like Bill Clinton, he is unlikely to even hint at a reconciliation with Mugabe unless the latter demonstrates in word and deed that he is what they call a libertarian.

For Mugabe, the avowed Marxist-Leninist, that is going to be a tall order. Stalemate seems a likely result. American presidents take their jobs seriously, but never as seriously as African presidents. The aspiring president in Africa will kill to get the job.

He will kill to keep it. The American president will cheat or try to cheat – as George W Bush did in 2000. On the day of his inauguration in 2001, one placard read Bush Cheated.

A Zimbabwean placard like that, after the 2002 presidential election, might have earned the carrier more than a bash on the head.

Presidential assassinations in the US are not necessarily associated with the winner's mode of victory. John F Kennedy had been in office for nearly three years when he was killed in 1963.

Nobody has ever suggested it was the manner in which he beat Richard M. Nixon that caused it. African presidents have fared far worse. More have been killed while in office than in the US.

Still, the US president, though powerful politically, is not rewarded as lavishly as the African president, who would normally be one of the highest-paid workers in the country.

The US president, by comparison, is not on a salary that would attract the CEO of Ford or General Motors to the job. Americans may respect their president, but they don't fear them. Africans fear their president, but don't respect him. Zimbabweans fear their president. The president inspires fear.

American mothers, not fathers, would love for their children to become president, if we are to believe this line I have always loved in Soliloquy in the musical comedy Carousel: He might be champ of the heavyweights or a fellow that sells G-blue or president of the United States. That would be all right too. In an aside, the man says his son's mother would love that, but he would not be president "unless he wanted to be". Perhaps the Americans appreciate the deadly risks involved in the job. But in 228 years of independence, only four presidents have been assassinated – Abraham Lincoln, James A Garfield, William McKinley and John F Kennedy. Since 1957, the number of African presidents assassinated is far higher than that. In Ghana and Nigeria alone, the number is staggering. If you count the number of presidents who died in exile, fearing assassination if they remained in their country, the number climbs even higher. Kwame Nkrumah, Mohammed Siad Barre, Mobutu Sese Seko and Idi Amin are among those who died in exile because if they had been in their countries they certainly would have been killed. Milton Obote (Zambia) and Mengistu Haile Mariam (Zimbabwe) dare not return to Uganda and Ethiopia, respectively. They know if they did they would be lynched. It's sad to say this of Nkrumah because he is something of an African icon. But that is the truth: if he had returned to Accra after the military coup which toppled him in 1966, there is little doubt that he would have been killed by the soldiers. Instead he went to his friend, Sekou Toure in Guinea, who died in office of natural causes. It's of some relevance to say that Toure was blamed for the death of the first secretary-general of the Organisation of African Unity, Diallo Telli of Guinea.

There is little profit to be gained in comparing the political, economic or social developments in the US with those in Africa. The US political system, while less advanced and less sophisticated than Europe's, is freer and fairer than Africa's. The Europeans find the US vulgar, loud and even uncouth. But some of this could be out of envy: America is wealthier and the people open and robust in their enjoyment of life and liberty. Africa, linked to the US and Europe through the umbilical cord of slavery and colonialism, may boast of its own centuries' old original political systems. But the ball game has changed completely in the third millennium. There is no chance of Africa returning to its roots, without being tragically entangled into total inertia and chaos. After the US presidential election, even Zimbabwe might learn that while calling the US president dirty names in New York might indicate a political machismo of sorts, what matters most is whether an African president can leave office to the beers and cheers — and not the spears and jeers — of his people.

CHAPTER EIGHT

What's Next: Optimism?

T   *he following commentaries were gathered when the rest of the world found out that President Bush was re-elected and they had no other choice but to move on. These valuable pieces were written by influential columnists from around the world, explaining what they really expected from the U.S, moving forward. These opinions can be used as a gauge to measure what has happened since November 2004. The following piece was published by the* Jordan Times *after the election results were known.*

Undoing the Damage

Jordan Times – Editorial.
Nov 5th 2005

For many around the world, the results of the US elections — the presidential, Senate and House races — dashed hopes of a leadership change in Washington that might have ushered in a new era in international relations.

But the reality is President George W. Bush has won reelection to another four-year term, and work needs to be done to convince his administration that with the frenzy of the polls behind us, there are many international policy issues that require a candid and thorough review.

Bush and the team he chooses to serve in his Cabinet now have an opportunity to take a long hard look at where the administration's policies have failed and why. They have much damage to undo, starting with the disregard with which so many in the international community have come to look at the US.

With statements of support already being made from individual countries such as France and international organisations like the European Union, many countries are looking to start on a new footing with the Bush camp. France, whose vehement opposition to the war on Iraq resulted in tense Franco-American ties, is talking about working "with the American administration on current crises: Iraq, the Middle East, Iran, the challenges of the African continent, to rebuild, to renovate transatlantic relations."

The international community has a right to call for such reassessment so that a sense of balance, universality and humanity is restored. That much Bush owes the world and the American public.

The first arena of redirection must be Iraq. Bush must make drastic adjustments in his Iraqi involvement and start formulating an exit policy from the war-torn country. He knows how divided his own people are on the issue. He knows well that the US-led war strained Washington's relations with so many important capitals. He should know too that superpower arrogance cannot sustain or nurture a free and democratic world.

He should heed the words of one of his own army officers in Baghdad who summed up the situation saying it made no difference who was in the White House, there was a job to be done, and it made no difference whether it was the US or the UN who would do it — Iraq could not be allowed to fall into civil war.

Bush II

The following editorial was published by Arab News, *one of the first and most prominent English dailies from Saudi Arabia.*

Bush II
Arab News – Editorial
Nov 5th 2004.

TUESDAY'S presidential election in the United States debunked the conventional wisdom in a number of ways. It attracted a record number of voters and, yet, contrary to conventional wisdom, the high turnout benefited the incumbent rather than the challenger. Conventional wisdom, this time backed by a large number of opinion polls, had predicted that President George Bush would either win with another wafer-thin majority or lose to his Democratic adversary, Sen. John Kerry. Early reports from exit polls appeared to confirm that by predicting a landslide for Kerry. By the time the day was over, however, Bush had collected more votes than anyone ever in US history. Later, conventional wisdom promised a long and arduous legal battle over the results. In the event, Kerry did the right thing by not unleashing the legal hounds. Having disproved conventional wisdom in so dramatic a manner, George W. Bush now has a unique opportunity to slaughter other clichés.

Bush's victory, accentuated by his party's gains in Senate, congressional and gubernatorial races, puts him in a stronger position than ever. That should help him revise his policies in Iraq, revive the Middle East peace process, and reformulate his Greater Middle East program within a more realistic framework with the help of regional allies.

Under Bush the United States has become politically and militarily involved in the Middle East as never before. It is, therefore, essential for Bush to gain a better understanding of the region and its many conflicts and problems. One way to do this would be for Bush to travel to a region which, but for a four-hour incursion into Baghdad airport last year, he has never visited. The second Bush administration also needs to discover, or rediscover, the importance of public diplomacy, cultural exchanges and people-to-people contacts.

The Middle East faces three important issues.

One is the Palestinian-Israeli conflict that dates back more than half-a-century. It did not come into being on Bush's watch and, most probably, will not be solved during his presidency either. But Bush has the merit of being the first American president to commit himself to the creation of a viable and genuinely independent Palestinian state. The whole region would be prepared to work with him and translate that pledge into reality.

The second problem in the region is Iraq's uncertain future. Bush's re-election is reassuring in the sense that he has said he would do what it takes to help Iraq rebuild what war has shattered. But Bush certainly needs to mobilize greater regional support for the Iraq project. The forthcoming conference in Sharm El-Shaikh, Egypt, provides a good opportunity for his administration to offer a new deal on Iraq.

The third major regional problem concerns the possibility of a nuclear arms race. The second Bush administration should go beyond exerting selective pressure and devise a broader policy that could lead to the creation of a nuclear-free zone in the Middle East. Despite claims, often echoed in the media, most nations in our region are prepared to work with the US in a common quest for solutions to these three key problems.

Having established his reputation as a war leader, Bush should use his second four-year term to become known as a peacemaker.

Network of Trust

The following editorial was sent to me from South Korea. Digital Chosun, *a very popular online magazine, ran this editorial just after the election. Chosun Network is one of the oldest news sources in South Korea, dating back to 1919 when it was founded as Chosun IIbo's foundation and declared the "Promotion of Neo-Civilization."*

Network of Trust
Digital Chosun – Editorial
South Korea
Nov 5th 2004.

The re-election of President George W. Bush gives advance notice that the United States in the forthcoming four years too will pursue a strong power-based foreign policy with priority placed on national security. That is the choice of the American people. The Korean government, based on a cool-headed perception of "Bush's United States," should heal the wounds the Korea-U.S. relations have sustained in recent years and re-establish a more mature alliance relationship. To that end, it should first of all grasp the other side's thinking and position accurately.

The U.S. presidential election this time around has clearly shown the changed conceptions of the American people following the Sep. 11 terrorist attacks. That the shocks from the calamitous terrorist attacks and intent to prevent them from recurring are carved in the minds of Americans much deeper than foreigners imagined has been confirmed. Though Bush's foreign policy has been criticized in the world community as being arbitrary unilateralism, the American people have judged it to be useful to safeguarding their security.

The "Bush doctrine" chosen by the Americans, while being based on moral absolutism spearheaded by American values, opts for offensive realism that does not exclude even pre-emptive strikes to fight against terrorism and thwart the proliferation of mass destruction weapons. In his acceptance speech, President Bush declared, "The United States will fight against terrorism with all its resources and strength mobilized." With the Republican Party gaining control of both the Senate and House of Representatives this time, furthermore, the Bush doctrine has secured a more powerful driving force.

How Korea will cope with the United States, which intends to adjust its world strategy and alliance relations while giving top priority to national security, is the key for the country. Contents of national interests may change according to times, and the quality of an alliance is bound to change thereby. If Korea and the United States adjust differences in their positions through a truthful and frank dialogue, while respecting their respective national interests, it will broaden the width and depth of their alliance relationship; there is no reason why conflicts should arise.

The Korean government should be more prudent in is relations with the United States. The ruling forces should refrain from advocating insubstantial "equality" and stirring up populist anti-American sentiment. They also should guard against falling into awkward nationalism over North Korea's nuclear development programs and North Korean Human Rights Act. Korea-U.S. cooperation is required on these issues more keenly than ever before; it would be conducive to not only peace on the Korean Peninsula but also to North Korea eventually. If Korea's ruling forces conduct diplomacy with the United States keeping their supporters with strong anti-American sentiment in their minds, it would be a short cut to sacrificing national interests in favor of politics. Efforts are also needed to correct the mistaken notion that the United States is a greater threat to security on the Korean Peninsula than North Korea.

It is also urgent to secure intimacy and trust between the heads of state of the two countries. Whether heads of state enjoy personal trust or not often affect national relations decisively. In parallel, various walks of life including the political circles should broaden the lower stream of diplomacy with the United States. A new horizon of relationships between the two countries could be sought from repairing and refining a "network of trust" between Korea and the United States.

George Bush's golden chance

Following Editorial was published in the South African daily The Star.

George Bush's golden chance
The Star
South Africa
November 5, 2004
By the Editor

Much to the chagrin of many other nations around the world, voters in the United States of America have given George W Bush another chance.

In a powerful statement, the electorate returned Bush for another four years with the highest number of votes ever for a US president.

And in the process they rebuffed a spirited challenge from the Democratic Party's candidate, John Kerry.

Bush's re-election has given him an opportunity to finish what he started and to mend the many broken fences around the world. We fervently hope multilateralism is a word he will grasp, and that it will become a basic part of his foreign policy.

The world would be eager to hear, for instance, how he plans to clean the mess in Iraq, which may yet make his election triumph a Pyrrhic victory.

In his victory speech this week he once again raised the hopes of millions of Iraqis for a better life and democracy after Saddam Hussein.

But if the spiral of violence in Iraq continues, it could destroy Bush's second term, just as the war in Vietnam bogged down and poisoned Lyndon Johnson's presidency from 1964 to 1968.

Also, he needs to complete the task of bringing lasting peace and democracy to Afghanistan, a place the US bombed and destroyed in search of the elusive Osama bin Laden. It would have been a travesty if Kerry was left with the task of restoring the human rights record of the US by putting an end to the shameful detention without trial of suspected terrorists at Guantanamo Bay.

As far as Africa is concerned, Bush has to see through the positive steps he took to help African leaders to fight poverty, underdevelopment and the HIV/Aids scourge. Africans also expect him to continue playing a leading role in getting the G8 countries to remain true to their promise to help African countries to help themselves, through the New Partnership for Africa's Development.

This is Bush's golden chance. Over the next four years he can redeem his administration and restore respect for the US as the world's only superpower.

We can't afford this trans-Atlantic squabble

The following article is from the International Herald Tribune *published in France. This article extensively describes the future of transatlantic relationships.*

Daniel S. Hamilton directs the Center for Transatlantic Relations at Johns Hopkins University. Joseph P. Quinlan is a Wall Street analyst and a fellow at the Center. They are the authors of Partners in Prosperity: The Changing Geography of the Transatlantic Economy.

We can't afford this trans-Atlantic squabble
Daniel S. Hamilton and Joseph P. Quinlan International Herald Tribune.
Friday, November 5, 2004.

A second term for George W. Bush is hardly the outcome Europe desired. But neither Europe nor America can afford four more years of strain.

The trans-Atlantic partnership was pushed to the brink during Bush's first term. Pundits opined that the trans-Atlantic partnership was doomed, that Europe and the United States no longer shared common vales and no longer needed each other. The crisis over Iraq, many proclaimed, was the prelude to a regrettable but inevitable European-American divorce.

Such loose talk, however, ignores two bottom-line economic facts upon which a fresh start may be built. First, despite the perennial hype about "big emerging markets," the economic relationship between the United States and Europe is by a wide margin the deepest and broadest between any two continents in history. Second, these ties that bind became stronger, not weaker, during Bush's first term.

Total trans-Atlantic trade in goods, for instance, jumped from $422 billion in 2000 to an estimated $475 billion in 2004 — a 12 percent increase. Moreover, European affiliates in the United States are presently enjoying a profits bonanza. After posting record earnings of $44 billion in 2003, the affiliates are on pace to earn a record $60 billion this year.

There is more European investment in Bush's home state of Texas alone than total U.S. investment in Japan and China put together.

European economies have never been as exposed to the North American market as they are today. Healthy trans-Atlantic commerce has literally become the economic lifeblood of some European companies, countries and regions. Without earnings growth in the United States, the last few years would have been far more difficult for many European companies.

Washington, meanwhile, should be relieved that rising anti-Bush sentiment across Europe has done little damage to the bottom line of Corporate America.

U.S. affiliate earnings in Europe have soared in recent years, despite trans-Atlantic acrimony over Iraq. The weak dollar has helped boost affiliate earnings to a record $82 billion last year, a rise of nearly 25 percent from the prior year.

Those earnings jumped another 29.2 percent in the first half of this year. In the second quarter alone, earnings totaled a record $25 billion, with strong gains reported in France and Germany — the two nations most opposed to the U.S.-led war in Iraq. U.S. companies continue to rely on Europe for half their total annual foreign profits.

This also makes Europe the most attractive overseas destination for U.S. foreign direct investment. Despite all the talk about U.S. firms decamping for China and India, more than 60 percent of total U.S. capital outflows of $609 billion this decade — $373 billion — has been sunk in Europe.

Last year, in the face of extremely strained relations, U.S. firms ploughed a near-record $100 billion into Europe. The surge has continued this year: U.S. investment to Europe soared by 50 percent in the first half of this year to $60 billion, and is on pace to reach $120 billion, a record high.

By a wide yet underappreciated margin, Europe is America's most important commercial market. The region is not only a critical source of revenue, it is also a key supplier of capital for the debt-stretched United States. European firms are key sources of employment and wages for U.S. workers, and essential sources of taxes for state and local governments.

A second Bush term offers both the United States and Europe an opportunity to build a new trans-Atlantic partnership grounded in the vital stake we have developed in the health of our respective economies.

At the June 2004 U.S.-EU summit, President Bush and European leaders declared their willingness to consider new initiatives to remove further barriers to trans-Atlantic commerce. In the wake of the president's victory, this agenda should become a high priority for both sides of the Atlantic.

The economic message of the past four years is simple: we literally cannot afford a trans-Atlantic divorce. A weaker trans-Atlantic bond would render Americans and Europeans less safe, less prosperous, less free and less able to advance either their ideals or their interests in the wider world.

The United States and the World: a New Start?

The following editorials are from the Daily Star *of Lebanon. These pieces should be considered the core of this little book, and encompass the spirit of what I am trying to achieve with this project.*

The United States and the world: a new start?
Editorial – Daily Star (Lebanon).
Nov 5th 2004.

George W. Bush has won his bid for re-election, and so the world must now resume dealing with an important issue: the exercise of U.S. power around the globe. The Middle East bears the brunt of the new American foreign policy of pre-emptive war, "regime change" and more-or-less forced reforms, so this issue interests us very much. The start of the new presidential term in January is an opportune moment for the U.S. and its friends, partners and targets around the world to rethink the negative and stressful aspects of their relationships, and build on and expand the positive ones.

Example: We now witness another classic case of how the U.S. should not conduct its foreign policy, in its sudden decision to go after the drug barons in Afghanistan as well as fighting the Taliban and other extremist militants there. Fighting terror and drugs simultaneously is sensible, of course, but the U.S. should not have spent years ignoring the obvious linkages between drugs and terror in Afghanistan, and should have worked harder to reduce demand for drugs within the U.S. Waging war on the supply side while insufficiently tackling domestic U.S. demand recklessly transforms this into only a "foreign" problem, instead of acknowledging it as an

American problem as well. Israel uses the same flawed approach when it expands settlements in occupied Palestinian lands and then attacks the Palestinians after accusing them of being terrorists for resisting colonization. This is not the way to make foreign policy in any country.

Solution: The U.S. can succeed in its diplomatic goals if puts the same energy into promoting the rule of law around the world as it puts into fighting terrorism through military means. The rule of law is not a nifty, self-contained, off-the-shelf democratic plan that the U.S. can impose on Iraq, Palestine, Afghanistan or any other land. It is a single, consistent set of values that applies to all countries, including the United States and Israel in their treatment of the Palestinians and others in this region. Middle Eastern and other countries are eager to work closely with the U.S. to promote a single standard of the rule of law; but they are determined to resist attempts to apply such a standard in a discriminating, whimsical manner. This is a major lesson of the experience of this Bush administration, and should be a guiding light for its policy in the next four years.

Engage the Next American President

I selected this editorial for many reasons. In my humble opinion, nothing has changed in the two years since President Bush was re-elected in 2004. If anything, the relationship between the U.S. and the Arab world has gone from bad to worse.

Wars have continued. People have died. Children have lost arms, legs, eyes…and the roaring sounds of tankers, bullets, and rockets continue. So what went wrong? This piece examines what the Arab world must do to enhance their relationship with the U.S.

Engage the Next American President
Daily Star – Lebanon
Tuesday, November 02, 2004

By Wednesday morning, barring legal challenges, Americans and the world should know whether George W. Bush or John F. Kerry is the next president of the United States. The verdict of the American people impacts directly, and often strongly, on the rest of the world, and this is particularly the case with Lebanon, Syria, Palestine and the rest of the Middle East.

The election of the next American president should be an opportunity that Arab leaders grab vigorously and quickly, in order to launch a new era of active political participation and engagement with American society. Security-level cooperation alone cannot form the basis of mutually beneficial and sustainable relations. If we do not engage the U.S. in a rational, useful manner, we are likely to be at the receiving end of more pre-cooked American ideological projects and assaults, such as Washington's push on UN Security Council Resolution 1559 and pressures on Iran. Syria in particular cannot afford to sit back and assume that Kerry would offer a new relation-ship, or Bush would change his policies. Damascus and other Arab capitals must actively explore new options for political partnerships with the U.S. on issues such as Palestine, Iraq, reform, and fighting terror and ending occupations.

A magical new era will not begin in the Middle East with the next president, unless the Arabs snap out of auto-pilot mode, and do the hard work they must do to change the direction of political trends in this increasingly violent region. The hard work includes exploring strategic options, offering mutually beneficial partnerships, lobbying the American scene, activating potential networks of Arab expatri-ates in the U.S., and building on existing ties in the worlds of busi-ness, academia, religion and civil society. Waiting for the next blow or threat from Washington is not an option.

Conclusion: War Fair?

W hen I migrated to America, one of the obvious things that surprised me was the lack of world news and the lack of prominence the American mass media outlets gave to world events. A clerk at my local post office told me that she didn't know a country called Sri Lanka existed until she saw my mailing envelope. I told her to watch BBC.

It would have been fine if 9/11 didn't happen, but not anymore. I don't think America and the rest of world can afford to have this huge chasm between them if we are sincerely willing to achieve global peace. It's extremely important to understand "why do they hate us?" It's extremely important to close the chasm.

This book is an attempt to help us close the gap, or at least a step towards crossing the chasm.

By concentrating on a single event (in this case: the Bush re-election), I thought I'd be able to gather a reasonable sample of opinions that people from around the world had about Americans. I also thought it's very important to gather these opinions in a particular time-frame and on a particular topic and most importantly in "raw form" to collect a measurable sample. The re-election of President Bush seemed like the perfect event. Every one of these rare pieces may have hidden messages when decrypted may give us valuable answers for most of the difficult questions that we have on the table. In addition, I also think these rare pieces may serve as a great collection for historians, journalists and political scientists who in some point in the future will find it extremely useful for their academic research.

But for me, personally, if this book can help one American reader re-think reaching out to the rest of the world may be a better option than taking a tough stand or launching war, then I will consider this project a success. If this book can help us re-think a conflict, then I will consider this project to be a major success. But above all, if this book can help us re-think the consequences of starting a war, and can save the life of one single child, then I will be the happiest person on earth.

A.J Muste, a leading non-violent social activist and Mahatma Gandhi, both captured these sentiments best:

"There is no way to peace. Peace is the way."

As we have already seen in Iraq, when wars are fought they become uncontrollable. Pre-emptive wars create civil wars that spread just like killer viruses. The shock, awe, and anger create distrust of an incredible magnitude that will only hurt our children. The residue that we leave on this planet will hurt our future generations.

In our modern times, I would like to add additional prose to A.J Muste's and Gandhi's words:

"There is no root cause for war. War is the root cause."

Thank you for reading this book.

Epilogue

*I*t just happened when the book went to press. The results of November 2006 mid-term elections were out and I had few days to gather the write-ups from around the world to include an epilogue to this book. The timing seemed perfect.

Have you ever tried to define the word epilogue? According to Princeton University WordNet: "The epilogue told what eventually happened to the main characters".

I would also like you to take note the respect and appreciation the world community has for American democracy.

No tears for bungling Rumsfeld. It wasn't so much the act of an ageing warrior falling on his sword to save his liege trouble, it was the act of a tribal chief sticking it in the back if an incompetent subordinate whose bungling had lowered the authority of the royal kraal.

- Daily Nation - Kenya

Martyn Turner, *The Irish Times*, Ireland.

It took six years, but American voters have demonstrated a belated understanding of what people virtually everywhere else have known for years: George W. Bush is a dangerous cowboy who needs to be restrained. What remains to be seen is whether the rebuke delivered by American voters will be reflected in US policies overseas, and there is little reason for optimism.

- Daily Star - Lebanon

It is a bewildering war out there in Iraq. US voters must have thought so too and for that reason, one of the "architects" of that war has had to cut and run without staying the course and finishing the job! No wonder he's been described as the "Fall Guy". Oh what a world!

- A R H Attah of Accra Mail (Ghana) writes on 'Poor, poor Rumsfeld'

The George Bush administration wanted a verdict (on Saddam) to coincide with the eve of Tuesday's mid-term elections. The Iraqi regime obliged. However, as the results have established, the judge's verdict made no difference to the verdict of America's electorate.

- Rickey Singh, Jamaica Observer

Frank Boyle, *Edinburgh Evening News*, Scotland.

Christo Komarnitski, *Sega*, Bulgaria.

A Democratic Congress will also produce some degree of restraint on further unilateral adventures. We may get some questions answered — but no more. Make no mistake about it, come 2008, this disastrous war and its devastating consequences will still be with us, still demanding a real debate and a real solution.
- Dr. James J. Zogby, President of Arab American Institute in Washington, DC

With Rumsfeld's departure, it remains to be seen if the scenario laid out by Bob Woodward in "State of Denial" will come to pass. Woodward cites a conversation between Cheney and an aide in which the vice president says, "Look, if Rumsfeld goes then they'll be after me, and next will be the President. You have to hold the line."
- Ahmad Faruqui, Daily Times - Pakistan

The Republican defeat testifies that American democracy holds those in power accountable in the peoples' court. The average American's voice counts. Democracy has the power to humble any arrogant man in the White House. It clips the wings of the powerful if they are naïve and dangerous. How many countries in the Muslim world can boast of a transparent and credible democracy where ballot power that actually works to hold the top man accountable?
- Nasim Zehra - Arab News

INDEX

Geneva, 10, 21, 69, 82
Georgia, 80
Germany, 62, 155
Ghana, 10, 12, 29, 115, 143, 166
Ghanaian Chronicle, 29
Ghanian Chronicle, 10
global community, 74
Google, 7
Gore, 17, 30, 49, 128
Guantanamo, 33, 70, 82, 153
Guatemala, 80
Guinea, 8, 143
Gwynne Dyer, 12, 92, 93
Gyasi, 10, 29

H

Hamas, 64
Hamilton, 13, 154
Harold Pinter, 10, 75
Hasan Bleibel, 12, 105
Hashemite, 35
health care, 25, 67, 79
Hiroshima, 72
Hispanics, 124, 125
Holmes, 34, 36
homosexuality, 68, 118
homosexuals, 55, 104, 124, 128

I

immigrant, 1, 8
India, 51, 155
Indian, 1, 48, 51, 64
Indonesia, 63, 80
Inquilab, 2
international community, 23, 24, 25,
    26, 69, 70, 71, 82, 116, 146
International Herald Tribune, 10, 13, 21,
    139, 154
Iran, 31, 35, 36, 58, 66, 146, 159
Iraq, 1, 3, 4, 6, 18, 24, 25, 26, 31, 32,
    33, 34, 35, 41, 42, 44, 45, 50, 51,
    54, 55, 56, 59, 60, 61, 62, 63, 69,
    70, 73, 74, 76, 82, 83, 85, 93, 119,

133, 140, 146, 147, 148, 152, 154,
    155, 158, 160, 162, 166
Ireland, 13
Irish, 129
Islamic, 15, 63, 64, 123, 126
Israel, 8, 10, 35, 45, 58, 62, 63, 121,
    122, 124, 125, 127, 128, 131, 133,
    158
Istanbul, 126

J

Jamaica, 11, 12, 65, 66, 117, 166
Jamaica Observer, 11, 12, 65, 117, 166
Jamaican Observer, 65
James Moore, 35
Jay S Bybee, 34
Jerusalem, 10, 122, 124, 125
Jerusalem Post, 10, 122, 124, 125
Jewish, 9, 24, 62, 64, 121, 122, 123,
    124, 125, 126, 127, 128, 129, 133
Jews, 8, 122, 123, 124, 125, 126, 127,
    129
Jihad, 126
jingoism, 32
Joe Lieberman, 128
John Ashcroft, 31, 34, 37, 123
John F Kennedy, 142
Jonathan Rosenblum, 10, 121, 122
Jordan, 12, 63, 145
Jordan Times, 12, 145
Jovial Rantao, 12, 101, 102
Julius Hansen, 11, 28, 106

K

Kansas, 52, 53
Karl Rove, 35, 97, 118, 122
Kashmir, 48, 64
Keeble McFarlen, 117
Keeble McFarlene, 12
Kennedy, 29, 142, 143
Kenya, 11, 47, 72, 107, 126, 164
Kerry, 9, 20, 38, 41, 48, 49, 54, 55,
    59, 66, 67, 68, 72, 93, 98, 102,
    103, 104, 110, 112, 113, 115, 116,
    123, 124, 125, 126, 127, 128, 129,